Organizational Infrastructure Complete Self-Assessment Guide

C000085367

The guidance in this Self-Assessment is based Infrastructure best practices and standards in k architecture, design and quality management. ᵢₕₑ guidance is also based on the professional judgment of the individual collaborators listed in the Acknowledgments.

Notice of rights

Trademarks

Table of Contents

About The Art of Service

The Art of Service, Business Process Architects since 2000, is dedicated to helping stakeholders achieve excellence.

Defining, designing, creating, and implementing a process to solve a stakeholders challenge or meet an objective is the most valuable role… In EVERY group, company, organization and department.

Unless you're talking a one-time, single-use project, there should be a process. Whether that process is managed and implemented by humans, AI, or a combination of the two, it needs to be designed by someone with a complex enough perspective to ask the right questions.

Someone capable of asking the right questions and step back and say, 'What are we really trying to accomplish here? And is there a different way to look at it?'

With The Art of Service's Standard Requirements Self-Assessments, we empower people who can do just that — whether their title is marketer, entrepreneur, manager, salesperson, consultant, Business Process Manager, executive assistant, IT Manager, CIO etc... —they are the people who rule the future. They are people who watch the process as it happens, and ask the right questions to make the process work better.

Contact us when you need any support with this Self-Assessment and any help with templates, blue-prints and examples of standard documents you might need:

http://theartofservice.com
service@theartofservice.com

Acknowledgments

This checklist was developed under the auspices of The Art of Service, chaired by Gerardus Blokdyk.

Representatives from several client companies participated in the preparation of this Self-Assessment.

In addition, we are thankful for the design and printing services provided.

Included Resources - how to access

Included with your purchase of the book is the Organizational Infrastructure Self-Assessment Spreadsheet Dashboard which contains all questions and Self-Assessment areas and auto-generates insights, graphs, and project RACI planning - all with examples to get you started right away.

How? Simply send an email to
access@theartofservice.com
with this books' title in the subject to get the Organizational Infrastructure Self Assessment Tool right away.

You will receive the following contents with New and Updated specific criteria:

• The latest quick edition of the book in PDF

• The latest complete edition of the book in PDF, which criteria correspond to the criteria in...

• The Self-Assessment Excel Dashboard, and...

• Example pre-filled Self-Assessment Excel Dashboard to get familiar with results generation

• In-depth specific Checklists covering the topic

• Project management checklists and templates to assist with implementation

INCLUDES LIFETIME SELF ASSESSMENT UPDATES

Every self assessment comes with Lifetime Updates and Lifetime Free Updated Books. Lifetime Updates is an industry-first feature which allows you to receive verified self assessment updates, ensuring you always have the most accurate information at your fingertips.

Get it now- you will be glad you did - do it now, before you forget.

Send an email to **access@theartofservice.com** with this books' title in the subject to get the Organizational Infrastructure Self Assessment Tool right away.

Your feedback is invaluable to us

If you recently bought this book, we would love to hear from you! You can do this by writing a review on amazon (or the online store where you purchased this book) about your last purchase! As part of our continual service improvement process, we love to hear real client experiences and feedback.

How does it work?
To post a review on Amazon, just log in to your account and click on the Create Your Own Review button (under Customer Reviews) of the relevant product page. You can find examples of product reviews in Amazon. If you purchased from another online store, simply follow their procedures.

What happens when I submit my review?
Once you have submitted your review, send us an email at review@theartofservice.com with the link to your review so we can properly thank you for your feedback.

Purpose of this Self-Assessment

This Self-Assessment has been developed to improve understanding of the requirements and elements of Organizational Infrastructure, based on best practices and standards in business process architecture, design and quality management.

It is designed to allow for a rapid Self-Assessment to determine how closely existing management practices and procedures correspond to the elements of the Self-Assessment.

The criteria of requirements and elements of Organizational Infrastructure have been rephrased in the format of a Self-Assessment questionnaire, with a seven-criterion scoring system, as explained in this document.

In this format, even with limited background knowledge of Organizational Infrastructure, a manager can quickly review existing operations to determine how they measure up to the standards. This in turn can serve as the starting point of a 'gap analysis' to identify management tools or system elements that might usefully be implemented in the organization to help improve overall performance.

How to use the Self-Assessment

On the following pages are a series of questions to identify to what extent your Organizational Infrastructure initiative is complete in comparison to the requirements set in standards.

To facilitate answering the questions, there is a space in front of each question to enter a score on a scale of '1' to '5'.

1 Strongly Disagree

2 Disagree

3 Neutral

4 Agree

5 Strongly Agree

Read the question and rate it with the following in front of mind:

**'In my belief,
the answer to this question is clearly defined'.**

There are two ways in which you can choose to interpret this statement;
1.   how aware are you that the answer to the question is clearly defined

2. for more in-depth analysis you can choose to gather evidence and confirm the answer to the question. This obviously will take more time, most Self-Assessment users opt for the first way to interpret the question and dig deeper later on based on the outcome of the overall Self-Assessment.

A score of '1' would mean that the answer is not clear at all, where a '5' would mean the answer is crystal clear and defined. Leave emtpy when the question is not applicable or you don't want to answer it, you can skip it without affecting your score. Write your score in the space provided.

After you have responded to all the appropriate statements in each section, compute your average score for that section, using the formula provided, and round to the nearest tenth. Then transfer to the corresponding spoke in the Organizational Infrastructure Scorecard on the second next page of the Self-Assessment.

Your completed Organizational Infrastructure Scorecard will give you a clear presentation of which Organizational Infrastructure areas need attention.

Organizational Infrastructure Scorecard Example

Example of how the finalized Scorecard can look like:

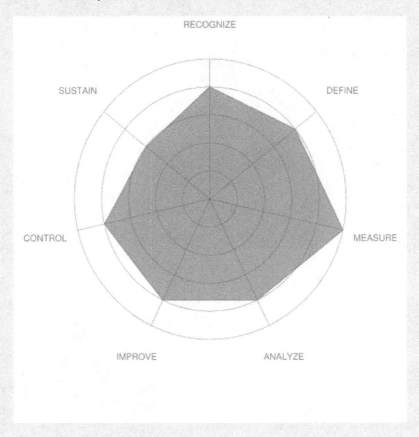

Organizational Infrastructure Scorecard

Your Scores:

BEGINNING OF THE SELF-ASSESSMENT:

CRITERION #1: RECOGNIZE

INTENT: Be aware of the need for change. Recognize that there is an unfavorable variation, problem or symptom.

In my belief, the answer to this question is clearly defined:

5 Strongly Agree

4 Agree

3 Neutral

2 Disagree

1 Strongly Disagree

1. What is the smallest subset of the problem you can usefully solve?
<--- Score

2. To what extent does each concerned units management team recognize organizational infrastructure as an effective investment?
<--- Score

3. Do you need to avoid or amend any organizational infrastructure activities?
<--- Score

4. Who needs to know?
<--- Score

5. What problems are you facing and how do you consider organizational infrastructure will circumvent those obstacles?
<--- Score

6. Do you need different information or graphics?
<--- Score

7. What tools and technologies are needed for a custom organizational infrastructure project?
<--- Score

8. Who needs to know about organizational infrastructure?
<--- Score

9. Whom do you really need or want to serve?
<--- Score

10. What is the problem or issue?
<--- Score

11. How do you recognize an objection?
<--- Score

12. Consider your own organizational infrastructure project, what types of organizational problems do you think might be causing or affecting your problem, based on the

work done so far?
<--- Score

13. What are the timeframes required to resolve each of the issues/problems?
<--- Score

14. Who else hopes to benefit from it?
<--- Score

15. What organizational infrastructure coordination do you need?
<--- Score

16. What organizational infrastructure capabilities do you need?
<--- Score

17. Are problem definition and motivation clearly presented?
<--- Score

18. How does it fit into your organizational needs and tasks?
<--- Score

19. Are there organizational infrastructure problems defined?
<--- Score

20. Think about the people you identified for your organizational infrastructure project and the project responsibilities you would assign to them, what kind of training do you think they would need to perform these responsibilities effectively?
<--- Score

21. Will a response program recognize when a crisis occurs and provide some level of response?
<--- Score

22. What organizational infrastructure problem should be solved?
<--- Score

23. Looking at each person individually – does every one have the qualities which are needed to work in this group?
<--- Score

24. Who needs budgets?
<--- Score

25. How are you going to measure success?
<--- Score

26. What does organizational infrastructure success mean to the stakeholders?
<--- Score

27. How are the organizational infrastructure's objectives aligned to the group's overall stakeholder strategy?
<--- Score

28. Who defines the rules in relation to any given issue?
<--- Score

29. How much are sponsors, customers, partners, stakeholders involved in organizational infrastructure? In other words, what are the risks, if organizational

infrastructure does not deliver successfully?
<--- Score

30. What is the extent or complexity of the organizational infrastructure problem?
<--- Score

31. What organizational infrastructure events should you attend?
<--- Score

32. What situation(s) led to this organizational infrastructure Self Assessment?
<--- Score

33. Are controls defined to recognize and contain problems?
<--- Score

34. Are there recognized organizational infrastructure problems?
<--- Score

35. What do employees need in the short term?
<--- Score

36. What are the organizational infrastructure resources needed?
<--- Score

37. Would you recognize a threat from the inside?
<--- Score

38. What is the problem and/or vulnerability?
<--- Score

39. Why the need?
<--- Score

40. Will new equipment/products be required to facilitate organizational infrastructure delivery, for example is new software needed?
<--- Score

41. What else needs to be measured?
<--- Score

42. Are your goals realistic? Do you need to redefine your problem? Perhaps the problem has changed or maybe you have reached your goal and need to set a new one?
<--- Score

43. Where is training needed?
<--- Score

44. What are your needs in relation to organizational infrastructure skills, labor, equipment, and markets?
<--- Score

45. How do you identify the kinds of information that you will need?
<--- Score

46. How are training requirements identified?
<--- Score

47. Why is this needed?
<--- Score

48. What should be considered when identifying available resources, constraints, and deadlines?

<--- Score

49. Which needs are not included or involved?
<--- Score

50. Who should resolve the organizational infrastructure issues?
<--- Score

51. What training and capacity building actions are needed to implement proposed reforms?
<--- Score

52. Is it clear when you think of the day ahead of you what activities and tasks you need to complete?
<--- Score

53. Are employees recognized for desired behaviors?
<--- Score

54. What creative shifts do you need to take?
<--- Score

55. What information do users need?
<--- Score

56. Are there regulatory / compliance issues?
<--- Score

57. When a organizational infrastructure manager recognizes a problem, what options are available?
<--- Score

58. What are the stakeholder objectives to be achieved with organizational infrastructure?

<--- Score

59. What do you need to start doing?
<--- Score

60. How can auditing be a preventative security measure?
<--- Score

61. As a sponsor, customer or management, how important is it to meet goals, objectives?
<--- Score

62. What would happen if organizational infrastructure weren't done?
<--- Score

63. How do you take a forward-looking perspective in identifying organizational infrastructure research related to market response and models?
<--- Score

64. How do you identify subcontractor relationships?
<--- Score

65. To what extent would your organization benefit from being recognized as a award recipient?
<--- Score

66. Which issues are too important to ignore?
<--- Score

67. What needs to be done?
<--- Score

68. Is the need for organizational change recognized?
<--- Score

69. Where do you need to exercise leadership?
<--- Score

70. Do you know what you need to know about organizational infrastructure?
<--- Score

71. Are you dealing with any of the same issues today as yesterday? What can you do about this?
<--- Score

72. Which information does the organizational infrastructure business case need to include?
<--- Score

73. What are the clients issues and concerns?
<--- Score

74. Does the problem have ethical dimensions?
<--- Score

75. Do you recognize organizational infrastructure achievements?
<--- Score

76. What needs to stay?
<--- Score

77. How many trainings, in total, are needed?
<--- Score

78. What resources or support might you need?

<--- Score

79. Are there any revenue recognition issues?
<--- Score

80. Have you identified your organizational infrastructure key performance indicators?
<--- Score

81. Are employees recognized or rewarded for performance that demonstrates the highest levels of integrity?
<--- Score

82. Is it needed?
<--- Score

83. Are losses recognized in a timely manner?
<--- Score

84. What are the expected benefits of organizational infrastructure to the stakeholder?
<--- Score

85. What activities does the governance board need to consider?
<--- Score

86. Can management personnel recognize the monetary benefit of organizational infrastructure?
<--- Score

87. Is the quality assurance team identified?
<--- Score

88. What prevents you from making the changes you

know will make you a more effective organizational infrastructure leader?

<--- Score

89. Are there any specific expectations or concerns about the organizational infrastructure team, organizational infrastructure itself?

<--- Score

90. Will organizational infrastructure deliverables need to be tested and, if so, by whom?

<--- Score

91. What is the recognized need?

<--- Score

92. How do you recognize an organizational infrastructure objection?

<--- Score

93. Does organizational infrastructure create potential expectations in other areas that need to be recognized and considered?

<--- Score

94. What extra resources will you need?

<--- Score

95. Who needs what information?

<--- Score

96. Did you miss any major organizational infrastructure issues?

<--- Score

97. How do you assess your organizational

infrastructure workforce capability and capacity needs, including skills, competencies, and staffing levels?
<--- Score

Add up total points for this section:
_ _ _ _ _ = Total points for this section

Divided by: _ _ _ _ _ _ (number of statements answered) = _ _ _ _ _ _
Average score for this section

Transfer your score to the organizational infrastructure Index at the beginning of the Self-Assessment.

CRITERION #2: DEFINE:

INTENT: Formulate the stakeholder problem. Define the problem, needs and objectives.

In my belief, the answer to this question is clearly defined:

5 Strongly Agree

4 Agree

3 Neutral

2 Disagree

1 Strongly Disagree

1. What are the boundaries of the scope? What is in bounds and what is not? What is the start point? What is the stop point?
<--- Score

2. Are accountability and ownership for organizational infrastructure clearly defined?
<--- Score

3. What is the scope of organizational infrastructure?

<--- Score

4. Have the customer needs been translated into specific, measurable requirements? How?

<--- Score

5. Is organizational infrastructure required?

<--- Score

6. Do you have a organizational infrastructure success story or case study ready to tell and share?

<--- Score

7. Is the current 'as is' process being followed? If not, what are the discrepancies?

<--- Score

8. Has anyone else (internal or external to the group) attempted to solve this problem or a similar one before? If so, what knowledge can be leveraged from these previous efforts?

<--- Score

9. Has/have the customer(s) been identified?

<--- Score

10. How have you defined all organizational infrastructure requirements first?

<--- Score

11. What sources do you use to gather information for a organizational infrastructure study?

<--- Score

12. How do you manage scope?
<--- Score

13. How do you gather organizational infrastructure requirements?
<--- Score

14. Do the problem and goal statements meet the SMART criteria (specific, measurable, attainable, relevant, and time-bound)?
<--- Score

15. What is out-of-scope initially?
<--- Score

16. What are the organizational infrastructure tasks and definitions?
<--- Score

17. How did the organizational infrastructure manager receive input to the development of a organizational infrastructure improvement plan and the estimated completion dates/times of each activity?
<--- Score

18. When are meeting minutes sent out? Who is on the distribution list?
<--- Score

19. If substitutes have been appointed, have they been briefed on the organizational infrastructure goals and received regular communications as to the progress to date?
<--- Score

20. What organizational infrastructure services do

you require?
<--- Score

21. What was the context?
<--- Score

22. Where can you gather more information?
<--- Score

23. Are there any constraints known that bear on the
ability to perform organizational infrastructure work?
How is the team addressing them?
<--- Score

24. Is the work to date meeting requirements?
<--- Score

25. Are the organizational infrastructure requirements
testable?
<--- Score

26. Are task requirements clearly defined?
<--- Score

27. What customer feedback methods were used to
solicit their input?
<--- Score

**28. Why are you doing organizational
infrastructure and what is the scope?**
<--- Score

29. Is there a critical path to deliver organizational
infrastructure results?
<--- Score

30. What gets examined?
<--- Score

31. Are approval levels defined for contracts and supplements to contracts?
<--- Score

32. What system do you use for gathering organizational infrastructure information?
<--- Score

33. What intelligence can you gather?
<--- Score

34. Is the organizational infrastructure scope manageable?
<--- Score

35. Has a team charter been developed and communicated?
<--- Score

36. What are (control) requirements for organizational infrastructure Information?
<--- Score

37. Who is gathering information?
<--- Score

38. Are there different segments of customers?
<--- Score

39. Is organizational infrastructure linked to key stakeholder goals and objectives?
<--- Score

40. How will variation in the actual durations of each activity be dealt with to ensure that the expected organizational infrastructure results are met?
<--- Score

41. Is the scope of organizational infrastructure defined?
<--- Score

42. Have all of the relationships been defined properly?
<--- Score

43. Has the improvement team collected the 'voice of the customer' (obtained feedback – qualitative and quantitative)?
<--- Score

44. What are the record-keeping requirements of organizational infrastructure activities?
<--- Score

45. In what way can you redefine the criteria of choice clients have in your category in your favor?
<--- Score

46. What are the tasks and definitions?
<--- Score

47. Is it clearly defined in and to your organization what you do?
<--- Score

48. What happens if organizational infrastructure's scope changes?
<--- Score

49. Is there regularly 100% attendance at the team meetings? If not, have appointed substitutes attended to preserve cross-functionality and full representation?
<--- Score

50. How would you define organizational infrastructure leadership?
<--- Score

51. What is in the scope and what is not in scope?
<--- Score

52. Is there a completed, verified, and validated high-level 'as is' (not 'should be' or 'could be') stakeholder process map?
<--- Score

53. How is the team tracking and documenting its work?
<--- Score

54. What information do you gather?
<--- Score

55. Will a organizational infrastructure production readiness review be required?
<--- Score

56. What critical content must be communicated – who, what, when, where, and how?
<--- Score

57. When is/was the organizational infrastructure start date?

<--- Score

58. Is special organizational infrastructure user knowledge required?
<--- Score

59. Are the organizational infrastructure requirements complete?
<--- Score

60. Has your scope been defined?
<--- Score

61. How do you manage changes in organizational infrastructure requirements?
<--- Score

62. How do you think the partners involved in organizational infrastructure would have defined success?
<--- Score

63. What is the context?
<--- Score

64. When is the estimated completion date?
<--- Score

65. What defines best in class?
<--- Score

66. What information should you gather?
<--- Score

67. What organizational infrastructure requirements should be gathered?

<--- Score

68. How often are the team meetings?
<--- Score

69. Is there a organizational infrastructure management charter, including stakeholder case, problem and goal statements, scope, milestones, roles and responsibilities, communication plan?
<--- Score

70. Does the team have regular meetings?
<--- Score

71. Has everyone on the team, including the team leaders, been properly trained?
<--- Score

72. Has the direction changed at all during the course of organizational infrastructure? If so, when did it change and why?
<--- Score

73. What are the dynamics of the communication plan?
<--- Score

74. Have all basic functions of organizational infrastructure been defined?
<--- Score

75. What is in scope?
<--- Score

76. Who defines (or who defined) the rules and roles?
<--- Score

77. What key stakeholder process output measure(s) does organizational infrastructure leverage and how?
<--- Score

78. Has a high-level 'as is' process map been completed, verified and validated?
<--- Score

79. Are all requirements met?
<--- Score

80. What baselines are required to be defined and managed?
<--- Score

81. What specifically is the problem? Where does it occur? When does it occur? What is its extent?
<--- Score

82. How do you catch organizational infrastructure definition inconsistencies?
<--- Score

83. How will the organizational infrastructure team and the group measure complete success of organizational infrastructure?
<--- Score

84. What scope do you want your strategy to cover?
<--- Score

85. Do you all define organizational infrastructure in the same way?
<--- Score

86. Has the organizational infrastructure work been fairly and/or equitably divided and delegated among team members who are qualified and capable to perform the work? Has everyone contributed?
<--- Score

87. What is the scope of the organizational infrastructure effort?
<--- Score

88. What would be the goal or target for a organizational infrastructure's improvement team?
<--- Score

89. Is data collected and displayed to better understand customer(s) critical needs and requirements.
<--- Score

90. Is there a clear organizational infrastructure case definition?
<--- Score

91. What is the scope of the organizational infrastructure work?
<--- Score

92. Is the team adequately staffed with the desired cross-functionality? If not, what additional resources are available to the team?
<--- Score

93. What are the organizational infrastructure use cases?
<--- Score

94. Is there a completed SIPOC representation, describing the Suppliers, Inputs, Process, Outputs, and Customers?
<--- Score

95. Is scope creep really all bad news?
<--- Score

96. How do you keep key subject matter experts in the loop?
<--- Score

97. How would you define the culture at your organization, how susceptible is it to organizational infrastructure changes?
<--- Score

98. Are audit criteria, scope, frequency and methods defined?
<--- Score

99. Is the organizational infrastructure scope complete and appropriately sized?
<--- Score

100. What are the requirements for audit information?
<--- Score

101. What are the rough order estimates on cost savings/opportunities that organizational infrastructure brings?
<--- Score

102. What is the definition of organizational infrastructure excellence?

<--- Score

103. Is the improvement team aware of the different versions of a process: what they think it is vs. what it actually is vs. what it should be vs. what it could be?
<--- Score

104. Have specific policy objectives been defined?
<--- Score

105. How does the organizational infrastructure manager ensure against scope creep?
<--- Score

106. What scope to assess?
<--- Score

107. Who is gathering organizational infrastructure information?
<--- Score

108. What is the worst case scenario?
<--- Score

109. Is organizational infrastructure currently on schedule according to the plan?
<--- Score

110. What constraints exist that might impact the team?
<--- Score

111. What are the Roles and Responsibilities for each team member and its leadership? Where is this documented?
<--- Score

112. Who are the organizational infrastructure improvement team members, including Management Leads and Coaches?
<--- Score

113. How do you manage unclear organizational infrastructure requirements?
<--- Score

114. What is the definition of success?
<--- Score

115. What are the core elements of the organizational infrastructure business case?
<--- Score

116. Has a project plan, Gantt chart, or similar been developed/completed?
<--- Score

117. How do you hand over organizational infrastructure context?
<--- Score

118. Are required metrics defined, what are they?
<--- Score

119. What sort of initial information to gather?
<--- Score

120. Has a organizational infrastructure requirement not been met?
<--- Score

121. How do you gather the stories?

<--- Score

122. What is out of scope?
<--- Score

123. What are the compelling stakeholder reasons for embarking on organizational infrastructure?
<--- Score

124. Are different versions of process maps needed to account for the different types of inputs?
<--- Score

125. How and when will the baselines be defined?
<--- Score

126. Who approved the organizational infrastructure scope?
<--- Score

127. How do you gather requirements?
<--- Score

128. Do you have organizational privacy requirements?
<--- Score

129. How do you build the right business case?
<--- Score

130. How can the value of organizational infrastructure be defined?
<--- Score

131. What is a worst-case scenario for losses?
<--- Score

132. Does the scope remain the same?
<--- Score

133. How was the 'as is' process map developed, reviewed, verified and validated?
<--- Score

Add up total points for this section:
_____ = Total points for this section

Divided by: _____ (number of statements answered) = _____
Average score for this section

Transfer your score to the organizational infrastructure Index at the beginning of the Self-Assessment.

CRITERION #3: MEASURE:

INTENT: Gather the correct data. Measure the current performance and evolution of the situation.

In my belief, the answer to this question is clearly defined:

5 Strongly Agree

4 Agree

3 Neutral

2 Disagree

1 Strongly Disagree

1. How frequently do you track organizational infrastructure measures?
<--- Score

2. Who should receive measurement reports?
<--- Score

3. What relevant entities could be measured?
<--- Score

4. Will organizational infrastructure have an impact on current business continuity, disaster recovery processes and/or infrastructure?
<--- Score

5. How can you manage cost down?
<--- Score

6. How do you quantify and qualify impacts?
<--- Score

7. What do you measure and why?
<--- Score

8. How can you reduce costs?
<--- Score

9. Are you aware of what could cause a problem?
<--- Score

10. How are measurements made?
<--- Score

11. How long to keep data and how to manage retention costs?
<--- Score

12. Which costs should be taken into account?
<--- Score

13. How do you focus on what is right -not who is right?
<--- Score

14. What is an unallowable cost?

<--- Score

15. Do you verify that corrective actions were taken?
<--- Score

16. How can you measure the performance?
<--- Score

17. When should you bother with diagrams?
<--- Score

18. When a disaster occurs, who gets priority?
<--- Score

19. How do you measure lifecycle phases?
<--- Score

20. What are you verifying?
<--- Score

21. How do you verify performance?
<--- Score

22. What evidence is there and what is measured?
<--- Score

23. How do you measure variability?
<--- Score

24. How do you stay flexible and focused to recognize larger organizational infrastructure results?
<--- Score

25. Have you made assumptions about the shape of the future, particularly its impact on your

customers and competitors?
<--- Score

26. What can be used to verify compliance?
<--- Score

27. What are the types and number of measures to use?
<--- Score

28. Was a business case (cost/benefit) developed?
<--- Score

29. What are the organizational infrastructure investment costs?
<--- Score

30. What are your key organizational infrastructure organizational performance measures, including key short and longer-term financial measures?
<--- Score

31. How will you measure your organizational infrastructure effectiveness?
<--- Score

32. What causes extra work or rework?
<--- Score

33. Where is the cost?
<--- Score

34. Is there an opportunity to verify requirements?
<--- Score

35. What harm might be caused?
<--- Score

36. What causes investor action?
<--- Score

37. What does losing customers cost your organization?
<--- Score

38. How do you verify and develop ideas and innovations?
<--- Score

39. What tests verify requirements?
<--- Score

40. Which measures and indicators matter?
<--- Score

41. What methods are feasible and acceptable to estimate the impact of reforms?
<--- Score

42. Who pays the cost?
<--- Score

43. Does a organizational infrastructure quantification method exist?
<--- Score

44. Are the units of measure consistent?
<--- Score

45. The approach of traditional organizational infrastructure works for detail complexity but is

focused on a systematic approach rather than an understanding of the nature of systems themselves, what approach will permit your organization to deal with the kind of unpredictable emergent behaviors that dynamic complexity can introduce?
<--- Score

46. What is the organizational infrastructure business impact?
<--- Score

47. What is the root cause(s) of the problem?
<--- Score

48. At what cost?
<--- Score

49. Are you able to realize any cost savings?
<--- Score

50. Do the benefits outweigh the costs?
<--- Score

51. How do you verify your resources?
<--- Score

52. Is the cost worth the organizational infrastructure effort ?
<--- Score

53. What are the operational costs after organizational infrastructure deployment?
<--- Score

54. Why do the measurements/indicators matter?
<--- Score

55. Do you effectively measure and reward individual and team performance?
<--- Score

56. What do people want to verify?
<--- Score

57. Has a cost center been established?
<--- Score

58. What would it cost to replace your technology?
<--- Score

59. How will measures be used to manage and adapt?
<--- Score

60. What are your customers expectations and measures?
<--- Score

61. Are the organizational infrastructure benefits worth its costs?
<--- Score

62. How can you reduce the costs of obtaining inputs?
<--- Score

63. What users will be impacted?
<--- Score

64. Do you have any cost organizational infrastructure limitation requirements?
<--- Score

65. How sensitive must the organizational

infrastructure strategy be to cost?

<--- Score

66. What disadvantage does this cause for the user?

<--- Score

67. How will effects be measured?

<--- Score

68. What are the strategic priorities for this year?

<--- Score

69. Have design-to-cost goals been established?

<--- Score

70. What would be a real cause for concern?

<--- Score

71. How do your measurements capture actionable organizational infrastructure information for use in exceeding your customers expectations and securing your customers engagement?

<--- Score

72. What measurements are possible, practicable and meaningful?

<--- Score

73. What does your operating model cost?

<--- Score

74. Are indirect costs charged to the organizational infrastructure program?

<--- Score

75. What is your decision requirements diagram?

<--- Score

76. Is it possible to estimate the impact of unanticipated complexity such as wrong or failed assumptions, feedback, etcetera on proposed reforms?
<--- Score

77. What are hidden organizational infrastructure quality costs?
<--- Score

78. Are organizational infrastructure vulnerabilities categorized and prioritized?
<--- Score

79. How do you prevent mis-estimating cost?
<--- Score

80. What is the total fixed cost?
<--- Score

81. Are missed organizational infrastructure opportunities costing your organization money?
<--- Score

82. How is the value delivered by organizational infrastructure being measured?
<--- Score

83. What could cause you to change course?
<--- Score

84. How do you control the overall costs of your work processes?
<--- Score

85. Does management have the right priorities among projects?
<--- Score

86. What causes innovation to fail or succeed in your organization?
<--- Score

87. What are your operating costs?
<--- Score

88. How will success or failure be measured?
<--- Score

89. How will your organization measure success?
<--- Score

90. How can a organizational infrastructure test verify your ideas or assumptions?
<--- Score

91. What is the cause of any organizational infrastructure gaps?
<--- Score

92. Have you included everything in your organizational infrastructure cost models?
<--- Score

93. How to cause the change?
<--- Score

94. Are supply costs steady or fluctuating?
<--- Score

95. What are the costs?
<--- Score

96. How will you measure success?
<--- Score

97. What are the costs and benefits?
<--- Score

98. Are there any easy-to-implement alternatives to organizational infrastructure? Sometimes other solutions are available that do not require the cost implications of a full-blown project?
<--- Score

99. What does verifying compliance entail?
<--- Score

100. Why a organizational infrastructure focus?
<--- Score

101. What details are required of the organizational infrastructure cost structure?
<--- Score

102. What are allowable costs?
<--- Score

103. What does a Test Case verify?
<--- Score

104. Are you taking your company in the direction of better and revenue or cheaper and cost?
<--- Score

105. What is measured? Why?

<--- Score

106. Where is it measured?
<--- Score

107. Where can you go to verify the info?
<--- Score

108. How do you verify and validate the
organizational infrastructure data?
<--- Score

**109. What are the organizational infrastructure
key cost drivers?**
<--- Score

**110. Are there competing organizational
infrastructure priorities?**
<--- Score

111. How do you verify the authenticity of the data
and information used?
<--- Score

112. How do you measure success?
<--- Score

113. Are actual costs in line with budgeted costs?
<--- Score

114. Do you have an issue in getting priority?
<--- Score

115. What causes mismanagement?
<--- Score

116. How are you verifying it?
<--- Score

117. Does the organizational infrastructure task fit the client's priorities?
<--- Score

118. Is a follow-up focused external organizational infrastructure review required?
<--- Score

119. Is the solution cost-effective?
<--- Score

120. When are costs are incurred?
<--- Score

121. How is performance measured?
<--- Score

122. Did you tackle the cause or the symptom?
<--- Score

123. Who is involved in verifying compliance?
<--- Score

124. Are there measurements based on task performance?
<--- Score

125. How frequently do you verify your organizational infrastructure strategy?
<--- Score

126. How do you verify if organizational infrastructure is built right?

<--- Score

127. What measurements are being captured?
<--- Score

128. What are the current costs of the organizational infrastructure process?
<--- Score

129. How do you verify the organizational infrastructure requirements quality?
<--- Score

130. How much does it cost?
<--- Score

131. Do you aggressively reward and promote the people who have the biggest impact on creating excellent organizational infrastructure services/ products?
<--- Score

132. What is your organizational infrastructure quality cost segregation study?
<--- Score

133. What could cause delays in the schedule?
<--- Score

134. Do you have a flow diagram of what happens?
<--- Score

135. Among the organizational infrastructure product and service cost to be estimated, which is considered hardest to estimate?
<--- Score

136. Are the measurements objective?
<--- Score

137. How are costs allocated?
<--- Score

138. What are your primary costs, revenues, assets?
<--- Score

139. What happens if cost savings do not materialize?
<--- Score

140. How do you aggregate measures across priorities?
<--- Score

Add up total points for this section:
_ _ _ _ _ = Total points for this section

Divided by: _ _ _ _ _ _ (number of statements answered) = _ _ _ _ _ _
Average score for this section

Transfer your score to the organizational infrastructure Index at the beginning of the Self-Assessment.

CRITERION #4: ANALYZE:

INTENT: Analyze causes, assumptions and hypotheses.

In my belief, the answer to this question is clearly defined:

5 Strongly Agree

4 Agree

3 Neutral

2 Disagree

1 Strongly Disagree

1. Where can you get qualified talent today?
<--- Score

2. When should a process be art not science?
<--- Score

3. What did the team gain from developing a sub-process map?
<--- Score

4. What are the organizational infrastructure design outputs?
<--- Score

5. How often will data be collected for measures?
<--- Score

6. Do you, as a leader, bounce back quickly from setbacks?
<--- Score

7. Is data and process analysis, root cause analysis and quantifying the gap/opportunity in place?
<--- Score

8. Has data output been validated?
<--- Score

9. Do your employees have the opportunity to do what they do best everyday?
<--- Score

10. Where is the data coming from to measure compliance?
<--- Score

11. How is the data gathered?
<--- Score

12. Did any value-added analysis or 'lean thinking' take place to identify some of the gaps shown on the 'as is' process map?
<--- Score

13. What are your current levels and trends in key measures or indicators of organizational infrastructure

product and process performance that are important to and directly serve your customers? How do these results compare with the performance of your competitors and other organizations with similar offerings?
<--- Score

14. How are outputs preserved and protected?
<--- Score

15. What organizational infrastructure metrics are outputs of the process?
<--- Score

16. How has the organizational infrastructure data been gathered?
<--- Score

17. Where is organizational infrastructure data gathered?
<--- Score

18. What are your current levels and trends in key organizational infrastructure measures or indicators of product and process performance that are important to and directly serve your customers?
<--- Score

19. What data do you need to collect?
<--- Score

20. Have the problem and goal statements been updated to reflect the additional knowledge gained from the analyze phase?
<--- Score

21. Are your outputs consistent?
<--- Score

22. What data is gathered?
<--- Score

23. Is there an established change management process?
<--- Score

24. What organizational infrastructure data should be managed?
<--- Score

25. What qualifications are needed?
<--- Score

26. What will drive organizational infrastructure change?
<--- Score

27. Do your leaders quickly bounce back from setbacks?
<--- Score

28. How much data can be collected in the given timeframe?
<--- Score

29. Is the gap/opportunity displayed and communicated in financial terms?
<--- Score

30. Who gets your output?
<--- Score

31. How do you identify specific organizational infrastructure investment opportunities and emerging trends?
<--- Score

32. What successful thing are you doing today that may be blinding you to new growth opportunities?
<--- Score

33. What are your organizational infrastructure processes?
<--- Score

34. Do quality systems drive continuous improvement?
<--- Score

35. Think about some of the processes you undertake within your organization, which do you own?
<--- Score

36. Has an output goal been set?
<--- Score

37. Do you have the authority to produce the output?
<--- Score

38. Who owns what data?
<--- Score

39. What types of data do your organizational infrastructure indicators require?
<--- Score

40. A compounding model resolution with available relevant data can often provide insight towards

a solution methodology; which organizational infrastructure models, tools and techniques are necessary?
<--- Score

41. How will the data be checked for quality?
<--- Score

42. What information qualified as important?
<--- Score

43. What are the processes for audit reporting and management?
<--- Score

44. What are evaluation criteria for the output?
<--- Score

45. What conclusions were drawn from the team's data collection and analysis? How did the team reach these conclusions?
<--- Score

46. What internal processes need improvement?
<--- Score

47. What do you need to qualify?
<--- Score

48. How does the organization define, manage, and improve its organizational infrastructure processes?
<--- Score

49. What is the organizational infrastructure Driver?
<--- Score

50. What quality tools were used to get through the analyze phase?
<--- Score

51. Is the required organizational infrastructure data gathered?
<--- Score

52. Was a cause-and-effect diagram used to explore the different types of causes (or sources of variation)?
<--- Score

53. How do you implement and manage your work processes to ensure that they meet design requirements?
<--- Score

54. What qualifications do organizational infrastructure leaders need?
<--- Score

55. Is the performance gap determined?
<--- Score

56. What controls do you have in place to protect data?
<--- Score

57. How is the way you as the leader think and process information affecting your organizational culture?
<--- Score

58. Who is involved with workflow mapping?
<--- Score

59. What, related to, organizational infrastructure processes does your organization outsource?
<--- Score

60. Do you understand your management processes today?
<--- Score

61. What does the data say about the performance of the stakeholder process?
<--- Score

62. How is organizational infrastructure data gathered?
<--- Score

63. What other jobs or tasks affect the performance of the steps in the organizational infrastructure process?
<--- Score

64. What is your organizations process which leads to recognition of value generation?
<--- Score

65. How do you measure the operational performance of your key work systems and processes, including productivity, cycle time, and other appropriate measures of process effectiveness, efficiency, and innovation?
<--- Score

66. What training and qualifications will you need?
<--- Score

67. Think about the functions involved in your

organizational infrastructure project, what processes flow from these functions?

<--- Score

68. Who will gather what data?

<--- Score

69. What are your outputs?

<--- Score

70. What are the disruptive organizational infrastructure technologies that enable your organization to radically change your business processes?

<--- Score

71. Do your contracts/agreements contain data security obligations?

<--- Score

72. What output to create?

<--- Score

73. What is the cost of poor quality as supported by the team's analysis?

<--- Score

74. What process improvements will be needed?

<--- Score

75. What qualifications and skills do you need?

<--- Score

76. Who qualifies to gain access to data?

<--- Score

77. What are the necessary qualifications?
<--- Score

78. Is there a strict change management process?
<--- Score

79. What is the Value Stream Mapping?
<--- Score

80. Can you add value to the current organizational infrastructure decision-making process (largely qualitative) by incorporating uncertainty modeling (more quantitative)?
<--- Score

81. Is there any way to speed up the process?
<--- Score

82. How do you ensure that the organizational infrastructure opportunity is realistic?
<--- Score

83. Do several people in different organizational units assist with the organizational infrastructure process?
<--- Score

84. Is pre-qualification of suppliers carried out?
<--- Score

85. What is the output?
<--- Score

86. What are the best opportunities for value improvement?
<--- Score

87. How do your work systems and key work processes relate to and capitalize on your core competencies?

<--- Score

88. Is the suppliers process defined and controlled?

<--- Score

89. Is the organizational infrastructure process severely broken such that a re-design is necessary?

<--- Score

90. How is the organizational infrastructure Value Stream Mapping managed?

<--- Score

91. Were any designed experiments used to generate additional insight into the data analysis?

<--- Score

92. What organizational infrastructure data do you gather or use now?

<--- Score

93. What were the financial benefits resulting from any 'ground fruit or low-hanging fruit' (quick fixes)?

<--- Score

94. Who is involved in the management review process?

<--- Score

95. Who will facilitate the team and process?

<--- Score

96. Have you defined which data is gathered how?
<--- Score

97. What organizational infrastructure data should be collected?
<--- Score

98. How many input/output points does it require?
<--- Score

99. What tools were used to generate the list of possible causes?
<--- Score

100. Have any additional benefits been identified that will result from closing all or most of the gaps?
<--- Score

101. How will the change process be managed?
<--- Score

102. Is the final output clearly identified?
<--- Score

103. How do you promote understanding that opportunity for improvement is not criticism of the status quo, or the people who created the status quo?
<--- Score

104. What is the oversight process?
<--- Score

105. Do staff qualifications match your project?
<--- Score

106. What were the crucial 'moments of truth' on the process map?
<--- Score

107. Are gaps between current performance and the goal performance identified?
<--- Score

108. Were Pareto charts (or similar) used to portray the 'heavy hitters' (or key sources of variation)?
<--- Score

109. Identify an operational issue in your organization, for example, could a particular task be done more quickly or more efficiently by organizational infrastructure?
<--- Score

110. Are all team members qualified for all tasks?
<--- Score

111. What kind of crime could a potential new hire have committed that would not only not disqualify him/her from being hired by your organization, but would actually indicate that he/she might be a particularly good fit?
<--- Score

112. How do you use organizational infrastructure data and information to support organizational decision making and innovation?
<--- Score

113. Are organizational infrastructure changes recognized early enough to be approved through the regular process?

<--- Score

114. What methods do you use to gather organizational infrastructure data?
<--- Score

115. Should you invest in industry-recognized qualifications?
<--- Score

116. Which organizational infrastructure data should be retained?
<--- Score

117. How will the organizational infrastructure data be captured?
<--- Score

118. What organizational infrastructure data will be collected?
<--- Score

119. Were there any improvement opportunities identified from the process analysis?
<--- Score

120. What are the revised rough estimates of the financial savings/opportunity for organizational infrastructure improvements?
<--- Score

121. What are the personnel training and qualifications required?
<--- Score

122. What are the organizational infrastructure

business drivers?
<--- Score

123. How was the detailed process map generated, verified, and validated?
<--- Score

124. Are you missing organizational infrastructure opportunities?
<--- Score

125. Record-keeping requirements flow from the records needed as inputs, outputs, controls and for transformation of a organizational infrastructure process, are the records needed as inputs to the organizational infrastructure process available?
<--- Score

126. What qualifications are necessary?
<--- Score

127. What are your key performance measures or indicators and in-process measures for the control and improvement of your organizational infrastructure processes?
<--- Score

128. What is the complexity of the output produced?
<--- Score

129. Was a detailed process map created to amplify critical steps of the 'as is' stakeholder process?
<--- Score

130. Did any additional data need to be collected?
<--- Score

131. Are all staff in core organizational infrastructure subjects Highly Qualified?
<--- Score

132. An organizationally feasible system request is one that considers the mission, goals and objectives of the organization, key questions are: is the organizational infrastructure solution request practical and will it solve a problem or take advantage of an opportunity to achieve company goals?
<--- Score

133. What tools were used to narrow the list of possible causes?
<--- Score

134. What is your organizations system for selecting qualified vendors?
<--- Score

135. What other organizational variables, such as reward systems or communication systems, affect the performance of this organizational infrastructure process?
<--- Score

Add up total points for this section:
_ _ _ _ _ = Total points for this section

Divided by: _ _ _ _ _ _ (number of statements answered) = _ _ _ _ _ _
Average score for this section

Transfer your score to the organizational infrastructure Index at

the beginning of the Self-Assessment.

CRITERION #5: IMPROVE:

INTENT: Develop a practical solution.
Innovate, establish and test the
solution and to measure the results.

In my belief, the answer to this
question is clearly defined:

5 Strongly Agree

4 Agree

3 Neutral

2 Disagree

1 Strongly Disagree

1. Are risk triggers captured?
<--- Score

2. Who will be using the results of the measurement
activities?
<--- Score

**3. What to do with the results or outcomes of
measurements?**

<--- Score

4. How are organizational infrastructure risks managed?
<--- Score

5. What error proofing will be done to address some of the discrepancies observed in the 'as is' process?
<--- Score

6. Do those selected for the organizational infrastructure team have a good general understanding of what organizational infrastructure is all about?
<--- Score

7. Are procedures documented for managing organizational infrastructure risks?
<--- Score

8. What tools do you use once you have decided on a organizational infrastructure strategy and more importantly how do you choose?
<--- Score

9. What are your current levels and trends in key measures or indicators of workforce and leader development?
<--- Score

10. What are the implications of the one critical organizational infrastructure decision 10 minutes, 10 months, and 10 years from now?
<--- Score

11. What improvements have been achieved?

<--- Score

12. How will you know that you have improved?
<--- Score

13. Is the scope clearly documented?
<--- Score

14. Where do you need organizational infrastructure improvement?
<--- Score

15. Do you have the optimal project management team structure?
<--- Score

16. If you could go back in time five years, what decision would you make differently? What is your best guess as to what decision you're making today you might regret five years from now?
<--- Score

17. Who do you report organizational infrastructure results to?
<--- Score

18. How can you improve performance?
<--- Score

19. What is the organizational infrastructure's sustainability risk?
<--- Score

20. Why improve in the first place?
<--- Score

21. Have you achieved organizational infrastructure improvements?

<--- Score

22. What were the criteria for evaluating a organizational infrastructure pilot?

<--- Score

23. At what point will vulnerability assessments be performed once organizational infrastructure is put into production (e.g., ongoing Risk Management after implementation)?

<--- Score

24. What is the implementation plan?

<--- Score

25. Was a organizational infrastructure charter developed?

<--- Score

26. Is there a high likelihood that any recommendations will achieve their intended results?

<--- Score

27. What is the risk?

<--- Score

28. Risk Identification: What are the possible risk events your organization faces in relation to organizational infrastructure?

<--- Score

29. Does the goal represent a desired result that can be measured?

<--- Score

30. How do you improve your likelihood of success ?
<--- Score

31. How will you recognize and celebrate results?
<--- Score

32. Which organizational infrastructure solution is appropriate?
<--- Score

33. Explorations of the frontiers of organizational infrastructure will help you build influence, improve organizational infrastructure, optimize decision making, and sustain change, what is your approach?
<--- Score

34. What organizational infrastructure improvements can be made?
<--- Score

35. How do you mitigate organizational infrastructure risk?
<--- Score

36. Who controls the risk?
<--- Score

37. How do you manage and improve your organizational infrastructure work systems to deliver customer value and achieve organizational success and sustainability?
<--- Score

38. How is knowledge sharing about risk

management improved?
<--- Score

39. How do you define the solutions' scope?
<--- Score

40. What tools were most useful during the improve phase?
<--- Score

41. Do you need to do a usability evaluation?
<--- Score

42. Are the key business and technology risks being managed?
<--- Score

43. Are the most efficient solutions problem-specific?
<--- Score

44. Is the organizational infrastructure risk managed?
<--- Score

45. What went well, what should change, what can improve?
<--- Score

46. Who controls key decisions that will be made?
<--- Score

47. What is the magnitude of the improvements?
<--- Score

48. How is continuous improvement applied to risk management?
<--- Score

49. How will you measure the results?
<--- Score

50. Who manages organizational infrastructure risk?
<--- Score

51. How do you go about comparing organizational infrastructure approaches/solutions?
<--- Score

52. What is organizational infrastructure's impact on utilizing the best solution(s)?
<--- Score

53. Is the organizational infrastructure documentation thorough?
<--- Score

54. Do vendor agreements bring new compliance risk ?
<--- Score

55. Are risk management tasks balanced centrally and locally?
<--- Score

56. What criteria will you use to assess your organizational infrastructure risks?
<--- Score

57. How do you decide how much to remunerate an employee?
<--- Score

58. Who are the key stakeholders for the

organizational infrastructure evaluation?
<--- Score

59. What actually has to improve and by how much?
<--- Score

60. Would you develop a organizational infrastructure Communication Strategy?
<--- Score

61. Is supporting organizational infrastructure documentation required?
<--- Score

62. Is the measure of success for organizational infrastructure understandable to a variety of people?
<--- Score

63. How risky is your organization?
<--- Score

64. What assumptions are made about the solution and approach?
<--- Score

65. What can you do to improve?
<--- Score

66. Is organizational infrastructure documentation maintained?
<--- Score

67. How do you link measurement and risk?
<--- Score

68. To what extent does management recognize

organizational infrastructure as a tool to increase the results?
<--- Score

69. Can you integrate quality management and risk management?
<--- Score

70. How do you measure improved organizational infrastructure service perception, and satisfaction?
<--- Score

71. Is the solution technically practical?
<--- Score

72. How do you keep improving organizational infrastructure?
<--- Score

73. What tools were used to evaluate the potential solutions?
<--- Score

74. How do you deal with organizational infrastructure risk?
<--- Score

75. Risk events: what are the things that could go wrong?
<--- Score

76. Can you identify any significant risks or exposures to organizational infrastructure third- parties (vendors, service providers, alliance partners etc) that concern you?
<--- Score

77. In the past few months, what is the smallest change you have made that has had the biggest positive result? What was it about that small change that produced the large return?
<--- Score

78. Do you cover the five essential competencies: Communication, Collaboration,Innovation, Adaptability, and Leadership that improve an organizations ability to leverage the new organizational infrastructure in a volatile global economy?
<--- Score

79. Who manages supplier risk management in your organization?
<--- Score

80. What strategies for organizational infrastructure improvement are successful?
<--- Score

81. For estimation problems, how do you develop an estimation statement?
<--- Score

82. What risks do you need to manage?
<--- Score

83. How can skill-level changes improve organizational infrastructure?
<--- Score

84. What area needs the greatest improvement?
<--- Score

85. Who makes the organizational infrastructure decisions in your organization?
<--- Score

86. Who should make the organizational infrastructure decisions?
<--- Score

87. Do the viable solutions scale to future needs?
<--- Score

88. How do you manage organizational infrastructure risk?
<--- Score

89. What is the team's contingency plan for potential problems occurring in implementation?
<--- Score

90. What do you want to improve?
<--- Score

91. When you map the key players in your own work and the types/domains of relationships with them, which relationships do you find easy and which challenging, and why?
<--- Score

92. How can you better manage risk?
<--- Score

93. Can the solution be designed and implemented within an acceptable time period?
<--- Score

94. How do you improve productivity?
<--- Score

95. What are the expected organizational
infrastructure results?
<--- Score

**96. Who do you report organizational
infrastructure results to?**
<--- Score

97. How scalable is your organizational infrastructure
solution?
<--- Score

98. How does your organization evaluate strategic
organizational infrastructure success?
<--- Score

99. What needs improvement? Why?
<--- Score

100. What resources are required for the improvement
efforts?
<--- Score

101. Is risk periodically assessed?
<--- Score

**102. How do you measure progress and evaluate
training effectiveness?**
<--- Score

103. Are you assessing organizational infrastructure
and risk?
<--- Score

104. What lessons, if any, from a pilot were incorporated into the design of the full-scale solution?
<--- Score

105. What are the affordable organizational infrastructure risks?
<--- Score

106. What are the concrete organizational infrastructure results?
<--- Score

107. Are events managed to resolution?
<--- Score

108. What were the underlying assumptions on the cost-benefit analysis?
<--- Score

109. How are policy decisions made and where?
<--- Score

110. Is any organizational infrastructure documentation required?
<--- Score

111. Will the controls trigger any other risks?
<--- Score

112. Have you identified breakpoints and/or risk tolerances that will trigger broad consideration of a potential need for intervention or modification of strategy?
<--- Score

113. Who will be responsible for documenting the organizational infrastructure requirements in detail?
<--- Score

114. Who are the people involved in developing and implementing organizational infrastructure?
<--- Score

115. organizational infrastructure risk decisions: whose call Is It?
<--- Score

116. Which of the recognised risks out of all risks can be most likely transferred?
<--- Score

117. Who will be responsible for making the decisions to include or exclude requested changes once organizational infrastructure is underway?
<--- Score

118. What tools were used to tap into the creativity and encourage 'outside the box' thinking?
<--- Score

119. How do you measure risk?
<--- Score

120. What practices helps your organization to develop its capacity to recognize patterns?
<--- Score

121. What is organizational infrastructure risk?
<--- Score

122. Are decisions made in a timely manner?

<--- Score

123. Risk factors: what are the characteristics of organizational infrastructure that make it risky?
<--- Score

124. How will you know when its improved?
<--- Score

125. How will you know that a change is an improvement?
<--- Score

126. How do the organizational infrastructure results compare with the performance of your competitors and other organizations with similar offerings?
<--- Score

127. Who are the organizational infrastructure decision makers?
<--- Score

128. Is the organizational infrastructure solution sustainable?
<--- Score

129. Where do the organizational infrastructure decisions reside?
<--- Score

130. How can you improve organizational infrastructure?
<--- Score

131. How can the phases of organizational

infrastructure development be identified?
<--- Score

132. For decision problems, how do you develop a
decision statement?
<--- Score

Add up total points for this section:
_ _ _ _ _ = Total points for this section

Divided by: _ _ _ _ _ _ (number of
statements answered) = _ _ _ _ _ _
Average score for this section

Transfer your score to the
organizational infrastructure Index at
the beginning of the Self-Assessment.

CRITERION #6: CONTROL:

INTENT: Implement the practical solution. Maintain the performance and correct possible complications.

In my belief, the answer to this question is clearly defined:

5 Strongly Agree

4 Agree

3 Neutral

2 Disagree

1 Strongly Disagree

1. What should you measure to verify efficiency gains?
<--- Score

2. Are operating procedures consistent?
<--- Score

3. What other areas of the group might benefit from the organizational infrastructure team's improvements, knowledge, and learning?

<--- Score

4. Is there a control plan in place for sustaining improvements (short and long-term)?
<--- Score

5. What is the standard for acceptable organizational infrastructure performance?
<--- Score

6. Does a troubleshooting guide exist or is it needed?
<--- Score

7. How do you encourage people to take control and responsibility?
<--- Score

8. What quality tools were useful in the control phase?
<--- Score

9. Do you monitor the effectiveness of your organizational infrastructure activities?
<--- Score

10. Is there documentation that will support the successful operation of the improvement?
<--- Score

11. Do the organizational infrastructure decisions you make today help people and the planet tomorrow?
<--- Score

12. How will the process owner verify improvement in present and future sigma levels, process capabilities?
<--- Score

13. Does organizational infrastructure appropriately measure and monitor risk?
<--- Score

14. What other systems, operations, processes, and infrastructures (hiring practices, staffing, training, incentives/rewards, metrics/dashboards/scorecards, etc.) need updates, additions, changes, or deletions in order to facilitate knowledge transfer and improvements?
<--- Score

15. What is the control/monitoring plan?
<--- Score

16. How do you spread information?
<--- Score

17. Are the planned controls working?
<--- Score

18. Who is going to spread your message?
<--- Score

19. What do you measure to verify effectiveness gains?
<--- Score

20. In the case of a organizational infrastructure project, the criteria for the audit derive from implementation objectives, an audit of a organizational infrastructure project involves assessing whether the recommendations outlined for implementation have been met, can you track that any organizational infrastructure project is implemented as planned, and is it working?

<--- Score

21. What is your theory of human motivation, and how does your compensation plan fit with that view?
<--- Score

22. Is there a standardized process?
<--- Score

23. Is there a documented and implemented monitoring plan?
<--- Score

24. What is the recommended frequency of auditing?
<--- Score

25. Have new or revised work instructions resulted?
<--- Score

26. Act/Adjust: What Do you Need to Do Differently?
<--- Score

27. Are controls in place and consistently applied?
<--- Score

28. Is a response plan in place for when the input, process, or output measures indicate an 'out-of-control' condition?
<--- Score

29. Can support from partners be adjusted?
<--- Score

30. Who is the organizational infrastructure process owner?

<--- Score

31. How is organizational infrastructure project cost planned, managed, monitored?
<--- Score

32. How might the group capture best practices and lessons learned so as to leverage improvements?
<--- Score

33. Will your goals reflect your program budget?
<--- Score

34. How do you plan on providing proper recognition and disclosure of supporting companies?
<--- Score

35. How will report readings be checked to effectively monitor performance?
<--- Score

36. Against what alternative is success being measured?
<--- Score

37. How will you measure your QA plan's effectiveness?
<--- Score

38. What key inputs and outputs are being measured on an ongoing basis?
<--- Score

39. Who controls critical resources?
<--- Score

40. Who will be in control?
<--- Score

41. Is reporting being used or needed?
<--- Score

42. Is a response plan established and deployed?
<--- Score

43. What is the best design framework for organizational infrastructure organization now that, in a post industrial-age if the top-down, command and control model is no longer relevant?
<--- Score

44. Will existing staff require re-training, for example, to learn new business processes?
<--- Score

45. Is knowledge gained on process shared and institutionalized?
<--- Score

46. What are the key elements of your organizational infrastructure performance improvement system, including your evaluation, organizational learning, and innovation processes?
<--- Score

47. How will the process owner and team be able to hold the gains?
<--- Score

48. Is the organizational infrastructure test/ monitoring cost justified?

<--- Score

49. Implementation Planning: is a pilot needed to test the changes before a full roll out occurs?
<--- Score

50. Is there a organizational infrastructure Communication plan covering who needs to get what information when?
<--- Score

51. What adjustments to the strategies are needed?
<--- Score

52. Where do ideas that reach policy makers and planners as proposals for organizational infrastructure strengthening and reform actually originate?
<--- Score

53. Can you adapt and adjust to changing organizational infrastructure situations?
<--- Score

54. What can you control?
<--- Score

55. What are the critical parameters to watch?
<--- Score

56. Is there an action plan in case of emergencies?
<--- Score

57. How will input, process, and output variables be checked to detect for sub-optimal conditions?

<--- Score

58. Has the organizational infrastructure value of standards been quantified?
<--- Score

59. How do controls support value?
<--- Score

60. How do senior leaders actions reflect a commitment to the organizations organizational infrastructure values?
<--- Score

61. Are the organizational infrastructure standards challenging?
<--- Score

62. How will new or emerging customer needs/requirements be checked/communicated to orient the process toward meeting the new specifications and continually reducing variation?
<--- Score

63. How do you select, collect, align, and integrate organizational infrastructure data and information for tracking daily operations and overall organizational performance, including progress relative to strategic objectives and action plans?
<--- Score

64. Is new knowledge gained imbedded in the response plan?
<--- Score

65. What are your results for key measures

or indicators of the accomplishment of your organizational infrastructure strategy and action plans, including building and strengthening core competencies?

<--- Score

66. Will the team be available to assist members in planning investigations?

<--- Score

67. Does the response plan contain a definite closed loop continual improvement scheme (e.g., plan-do-check-act)?

<--- Score

68. What should the next improvement project be that is related to organizational infrastructure?

<--- Score

69. Are documented procedures clear and easy to follow for the operators?

<--- Score

70. Are the planned controls in place?

<--- Score

71. Does job training on the documented procedures need to be part of the process team's education and training?

<--- Score

72. What are you attempting to measure/monitor?

<--- Score

73. What are customers monitoring?

<--- Score

74. What do your reports reflect?
<--- Score

75. Are you measuring, monitoring and predicting organizational infrastructure activities to optimize operations and profitability, and enhancing outcomes?
<--- Score

76. Are pertinent alerts monitored, analyzed and distributed to appropriate personnel?
<--- Score

77. What is your plan to assess your security risks?
<--- Score

78. Are there documented procedures?
<--- Score

79. How will the day-to-day responsibilities for monitoring and continual improvement be transferred from the improvement team to the process owner?
<--- Score

80. Is there a transfer of ownership and knowledge to process owner and process team tasked with the responsibilities.
<--- Score

81. Are suggested corrective/restorative actions indicated on the response plan for known causes to problems that might surface?
<--- Score

82. What are the known security controls?
<--- Score

83. You may have created your quality measures at a time when you lacked resources, technology wasn't up to the required standard, or low service levels were the industry norm. Have those circumstances changed?
<--- Score

84. Is there a recommended audit plan for routine surveillance inspections of organizational infrastructure's gains?
<--- Score

85. How is change control managed?
<--- Score

86. How will organizational infrastructure decisions be made and monitored?
<--- Score

87. Who sets the organizational infrastructure standards?
<--- Score

88. How do you plan for the cost of succession?
<--- Score

89. Who has control over resources?
<--- Score

90. Do you monitor the organizational infrastructure decisions made and fine tune them as they evolve?
<--- Score

91. Are new process steps, standards, and documentation ingrained into normal operations?
<--- Score

92. How do your controls stack up?
<--- Score

93. Does the organizational infrastructure performance meet the customer's requirements?
<--- Score

94. How can you best use all of your knowledge repositories to enhance learning and sharing?
<--- Score

95. How do you establish and deploy modified action plans if circumstances require a shift in plans and rapid execution of new plans?
<--- Score

96. How likely is the current organizational infrastructure plan to come in on schedule or on budget?
<--- Score

97. What organizational infrastructure standards are applicable?
<--- Score

98. Will any special training be provided for results interpretation?
<--- Score

99. Has the improved process and its steps been standardized?
<--- Score

Add up total points for this section:
_____ = Total points for this section

Divided by: _____ (number of
statements answered) = _____
Average score for this section

Transfer your score to the
organizational infrastructure Index at
the beginning of the Self-Assessment.

CRITERION #7: SUSTAIN:

INTENT: Retain the benefits.

In my belief, the answer to this
question is clearly defined:

5 Strongly Agree

4 Agree

3 Neutral

2 Disagree

1 Strongly Disagree

1. What are you trying to prove to yourself, and how might it be hijacking your life and business success?
<--- Score

2. Did your employees make progress today?
<--- Score

3. What must you excel at?
<--- Score

4. Who is the main stakeholder, with ultimate

responsibility for driving organizational infrastructure forward?

<--- Score

5. Why is it important to have senior management support for a organizational infrastructure project?

<--- Score

6. What is an unauthorized commitment?

<--- Score

7. What is the source of the strategies for organizational infrastructure strengthening and reform?

<--- Score

8. What is the range of capabilities?

<--- Score

9. If there were zero limitations, what would you do differently?

<--- Score

10. How important is organizational infrastructure to the user organizations mission?

<--- Score

11. What are the success criteria that will indicate that organizational infrastructure objectives have been met and the benefits delivered?

<--- Score

12. How do you lead with organizational infrastructure in mind?

<--- Score

13. What are the long-term organizational infrastructure goals?
<--- Score

14. Why should people listen to you?
<--- Score

15. How will you insure seamless interoperability of organizational infrastructure moving forward?
<--- Score

16. Are all key stakeholders present at all Structured Walkthroughs?
<--- Score

17. Which organizational infrastructure goals are the most important?
<--- Score

18. What is your BATNA (best alternative to a negotiated agreement)?
<--- Score

19. If you were responsible for initiating and implementing major changes in your organization, what steps might you take to ensure acceptance of those changes?
<--- Score

20. Who is responsible for ensuring appropriate resources (time, people and money) are allocated to organizational infrastructure?
<--- Score

21. What will be the consequences to the stakeholder

(financial, reputation etc) if organizational infrastructure does not go ahead or fails to deliver the objectives?

<--- Score

22. Who is on the team?

<--- Score

23. What business benefits will organizational infrastructure goals deliver if achieved?

<--- Score

24. Are you making progress, and are you making progress as organizational infrastructure leaders?

<--- Score

25. Are the criteria for selecting recommendations stated?

<--- Score

26. How do you keep records, of what?

<--- Score

27. What knowledge, skills and characteristics mark a good organizational infrastructure project manager?

<--- Score

28. What is the estimated value of the project?

<--- Score

29. Who uses your product in ways you never expected?

<--- Score

30. Who are the key stakeholders?

<--- Score

31. What projects are going on in the organization today, and what resources are those projects using from the resource pools?
<--- Score

32. How will you ensure you get what you expected?
<--- Score

33. What trophy do you want on your mantle?
<--- Score

34. How do you proactively clarify deliverables and organizational infrastructure quality expectations?
<--- Score

35. What are the challenges?
<--- Score

36. Ask yourself: how would you do this work if you only had one staff member to do it?
<--- Score

37. What is the craziest thing you can do?
<--- Score

38. Instead of going to current contacts for new ideas, what if you reconnected with dormant contacts-- the people you used to know? If you were going reactivate a dormant tie, who would it be?
<--- Score

39. How do you assess the organizational infrastructure pitfalls that are inherent in

implementing it?
<--- Score

40. How can you negotiate organizational infrastructure successfully with a stubborn boss, an irate client, or a deceitful coworker?
<--- Score

41. What trouble can you get into?
<--- Score

42. What unique value proposition (UVP) do you offer?
<--- Score

43. How do you foster innovation?
<--- Score

44. Are you satisfied with your current role? If not, what is missing from it?
<--- Score

45. If no one would ever find out about your accomplishments, how would you lead differently?
<--- Score

46. At what moment would you think; Will I get fired?
<--- Score

47. How much does organizational infrastructure help?
<--- Score

48. Do you have enough freaky customers in your portfolio pushing you to the limit day in and day out?
<--- Score

49. What is the kind of project structure that would be appropriate for your organizational infrastructure project, should it be formal and complex, or can it be less formal and relatively simple?
<--- Score

50. Operational - will it work?
<--- Score

51. What is the recommended frequency of auditing?
<--- Score

52. What could happen if you do not do it?
<--- Score

53. What is effective organizational infrastructure?
<--- Score

54. What is it like to work for you?
<--- Score

55. Do you see more potential in people than they do in themselves?
<--- Score

56. How can you become more high-tech but still be high touch?
<--- Score

57. What are the business goals organizational infrastructure is aiming to achieve?
<--- Score

58. What stupid rule would you most like to kill?
<--- Score

59. Do organizational infrastructure rules make a reasonable demand on a users capabilities?
<--- Score

60. How likely is it that a customer would recommend your company to a friend or colleague?
<--- Score

61. If you had to rebuild your organization without any traditional competitive advantages (i.e., no killer technology, promising research, innovative product/ service delivery model, etcetera), how would your people have to approach their work and collaborate together in order to create the necessary conditions for success?
<--- Score

62. Are you changing as fast as the world around you?
<--- Score

63. What should you stop doing?
<--- Score

64. Who are four people whose careers you have enhanced?
<--- Score

65. What are the usability implications of organizational infrastructure actions?
<--- Score

66. Do you have past organizational infrastructure successes?
<--- Score

67. What one word do you want to own in the minds of your customers, employees, and partners?
<--- Score

68. How much contingency will be available in the budget?
<--- Score

69. What threat is organizational infrastructure addressing?
<--- Score

70. Do you say no to customers for no reason?
<--- Score

71. Is organizational infrastructure dependent on the successful delivery of a current project?
<--- Score

72. Do you think you know, or do you know you know ?
<--- Score

73. What is the funding source for this project?
<--- Score

74. What is your competitive advantage?
<--- Score

75. Which individuals, teams or departments will be involved in organizational infrastructure?
<--- Score

76. What role does communication play in the success or failure of a organizational infrastructure

project?
<--- Score

77. Who have you, as a company, historically been when you've been at your best?
<--- Score

78. Are the assumptions believable and achievable?
<--- Score

79. Can you break it down?
<--- Score

80. How do you set organizational infrastructure stretch targets and how do you get people to not only participate in setting these stretch targets but also that they strive to achieve these?
<--- Score

81. If you find that you havent accomplished one of the goals for one of the steps of the organizational infrastructure strategy, what will you do to fix it?
<--- Score

82. How do you foster the skills, knowledge, talents, attributes, and characteristics you want to have?
<--- Score

83. Who do you think the world wants your organization to be?
<--- Score

84. How do you stay inspired?
<--- Score

85. Which functions and people interact with the supplier and or customer?
<--- Score

86. How do you listen to customers to obtain actionable information?
<--- Score

87. How is implementation research currently incorporated into each of your goals?
<--- Score

88. How do you create buy-in?
<--- Score

89. Is a organizational infrastructure team work effort in place?
<--- Score

90. Can the schedule be done in the given time?
<--- Score

91. How do you transition from the baseline to the target?
<--- Score

92. Can you maintain your growth without detracting from the factors that have contributed to your success?
<--- Score

93. Who, on the executive team or the board, has spoken to a customer recently?
<--- Score

94. When information truly is ubiquitous, when reach and connectivity are completely global, when computing resources are infinite, and when a whole new set of impossibilities are not only possible, but happening, what will that do to your business?
<--- Score

95. How do you keep the momentum going?
<--- Score

96. Is the organizational infrastructure organization completing tasks effectively and efficiently?
<--- Score

97. In retrospect, of the projects that you pulled the plug on, what percent do you wish had been allowed to keep going, and what percent do you wish had ended earlier?
<--- Score

98. Who is responsible for organizational infrastructure?
<--- Score

99. Is it economical; do you have the time and money?
<--- Score

100. Are assumptions made in organizational infrastructure stated explicitly?
<--- Score

101. Who will provide the final approval of organizational infrastructure deliverables?
<--- Score

102. Is your basic point _____ or _____?
<--- Score

103. How do customers see your organization?
<--- Score

104. Why is organizational infrastructure important for you now?
<--- Score

105. How do you maintain organizational infrastructure's Integrity?
<--- Score

106. Do you think organizational infrastructure accomplishes the goals you expect it to accomplish?
<--- Score

107. How long will it take to change?
<--- Score

108. Is maximizing organizational infrastructure protection the same as minimizing organizational infrastructure loss?
<--- Score

109. If you do not follow, then how to lead?
<--- Score

110. How do you know if you are successful?
<--- Score

111. What are the key enablers to make this organizational infrastructure move?
<--- Score

112. If your customer were your grandmother, would you tell her to buy what you're selling?
<--- Score

113. What are the potential basics of organizational infrastructure fraud?
<--- Score

114. What is the overall business strategy?
<--- Score

115. How do you deal with organizational infrastructure changes?
<--- Score

116. Why do and why don't your customers like your organization?
<--- Score

117. Why will customers want to buy your organizations products/services?
<--- Score

118. Is there any existing organizational infrastructure governance structure?
<--- Score

119. If you got fired and a new hire took your place, what would she do different?
<--- Score

120. How will you know that the organizational infrastructure project has been successful?
<--- Score

121. How do you engage the workforce, in addition to

satisfying them?

<--- Score

122. Are you paying enough attention to the partners your company depends on to succeed?

<--- Score

123. How do you determine the key elements that affect organizational infrastructure workforce satisfaction, how are these elements determined for different workforce groups and segments?

<--- Score

124. What was the last experiment you ran?

<--- Score

125. Do you have the right people on the bus?

<--- Score

126. Marketing budgets are tighter, consumers are more skeptical, and social media has changed forever the way we talk about organizational infrastructure, how do you gain traction?

<--- Score

127. How do you provide a safe environment -physically and emotionally?

<--- Score

128. What are the essentials of internal organizational infrastructure management?

<--- Score

129. Is there a work around that you can use?

<--- Score

130. What happens when a new employee joins the organization?
<--- Score

131. How do you track customer value, profitability or financial return, organizational success, and sustainability?
<--- Score

132. How do you accomplish your long range organizational infrastructure goals?
<--- Score

133. What would have to be true for the option on the table to be the best possible choice?
<--- Score

134. How will you motivate the stakeholders with the least vested interest?
<--- Score

135. In the past year, what have you done (or could you have done) to increase the accurate perception of your company/brand as ethical and honest?
<--- Score

136. What organizational infrastructure skills are most important?
<--- Score

137. Who do we want your customers to become?
<--- Score

138. Who else should you help?
<--- Score

139. How do you cross-sell and up-sell your organizational infrastructure success?
<--- Score

140. What does your signature ensure?
<--- Score

141. Do you have the right capabilities and capacities?
<--- Score

142. To whom do you add value?
<--- Score

143. Do you have an implicit bias for capital investments over people investments?
<--- Score

144. What are the barriers to increased organizational infrastructure production?
<--- Score

145. How do you go about securing organizational infrastructure?
<--- Score

146. What would you recommend your friend do if he/she were facing this dilemma?
<--- Score

147. Who will manage the integration of tools?
<--- Score

148. What is the overall talent health of your organization as a whole at senior levels, and for each organization reporting to a member of the Senior Leadership Team?

<--- Score

149. How can you become the company that would put you out of business?
<--- Score

150. In a project to restructure organizational infrastructure outcomes, which stakeholders would you involve?
<--- Score

151. Will it be accepted by users?
<--- Score

152. How do you govern and fulfill your societal responsibilities?
<--- Score

153. How are you doing compared to your industry?
<--- Score

154. How do you manage organizational infrastructure Knowledge Management (KM)?
<--- Score

155. Do you know what you are doing? And who do you call if you don't?
<--- Score

156. Where can you break convention?
<--- Score

157. How do senior leaders deploy your organizations vision and values through your leadership system, to the workforce, to key suppliers and partners, and to customers and

other stakeholders, as appropriate?
<--- Score

158. What are your personal philosophies regarding organizational infrastructure and how do they influence your work?
<--- Score

159. Are you relevant? Will you be relevant five years from now? Ten?
<--- Score

160. What are your most important goals for the strategic organizational infrastructure objectives?
<--- Score

161. Would you rather sell to knowledgeable and informed customers or to uninformed customers?
<--- Score

162. Will there be any necessary staff changes (redundancies or new hires)?
<--- Score

163. Think of your organizational infrastructure project, what are the main functions?
<--- Score

164. What is your formula for success in organizational infrastructure ?
<--- Score

165. If you weren't already in this business, would you enter it today? And if not, what are you going to do about it?
<--- Score

166. What have been your experiences in defining long range organizational infrastructure goals?
<--- Score

167. Are you maintaining a past–present–future perspective throughout the organizational infrastructure discussion?
<--- Score

168. Who do you want your customers to become?
<--- Score

169. How can you incorporate support to ensure safe and effective use of organizational infrastructure into the services that you provide?
<--- Score

170. What are specific organizational infrastructure rules to follow?
<--- Score

171. Is your strategy driving your strategy? Or is the way in which you allocate resources driving your strategy?
<--- Score

172. How do you make it meaningful in connecting organizational infrastructure with what users do day-to-day?
<--- Score

173. What management system can you use to leverage the organizational infrastructure experience, ideas, and concerns of the people closest to the work to be done?

<--- Score

174. Are your responses positive or negative?
<--- Score

175. Whose voice (department, ethnic group, women, older workers, etc) might you have missed hearing from in your company, and how might you amplify this voice to create positive momentum for your business?
<--- Score

176. What happens if you do not have enough funding?
<--- Score

177. What are current organizational infrastructure paradigms?
<--- Score

178. What you are going to do to affect the numbers?
<--- Score

179. Are you using a design thinking approach and integrating Innovation, organizational infrastructure Experience, and Brand Value?
<--- Score

180. What counts that you are not counting?
<--- Score

181. Political -is anyone trying to undermine this project?
<--- Score

182. What is something you believe that nearly no one

agrees with you on?
<--- Score

183. What are internal and external organizational infrastructure relations?
<--- Score

184. What current systems have to be understood and/or changed?
<--- Score

185. What is a feasible sequencing of reform initiatives over time?
<--- Score

186. What is your question? Why?
<--- Score

187. How do you ensure that implementations of organizational infrastructure products are done in a way that ensures safety?
<--- Score

188. What are the rules and assumptions your industry operates under? What if the opposite were true?
<--- Score

189. Why not do organizational infrastructure?
<--- Score

190. Are you / should you be revolutionary or evolutionary?
<--- Score

191. What is your organizational infrastructure strategy?

<--- Score

192. What is the purpose of organizational infrastructure in relation to the mission?
<--- Score

193. Has implementation been effective in reaching specified objectives so far?
<--- Score

194. Why should you adopt a organizational infrastructure framework?
<--- Score

195. Whom among your colleagues do you trust, and for what?
<--- Score

196. What relationships among organizational infrastructure trends do you perceive?
<--- Score

197. Do you feel that more should be done in the organizational infrastructure area?
<--- Score

198. Who will be responsible for deciding whether organizational infrastructure goes ahead or not after the initial investigations?
<--- Score

199. If you had to leave your organization for a year and the only communication you could have with employees/colleagues was a single paragraph, what would you write?
<--- Score

200. What are you challenging?
<--- Score

201. Who are your customers?
<--- Score

Add up total points for this section:
_____ = Total points for this section

Divided by: _____ (number of
statements answered) = _____
Average score for this section

Transfer your score to the
organizational infrastructure Index at
the beginning of the Self-Assessment.

Organizational Infrastructure and Managing Projects, Criteria for Project Managers:

1.0 Initiating Process Group: Organizational Infrastructure

1. Information sharing?

2. Were sponsors and decision makers available when needed outside regularly scheduled meetings?

3. Based on your Organizational Infrastructure project communication management plan, what worked well?

4. What are the constraints?

5. Are there resources to maintain and support the outcome of the Organizational Infrastructure project?

6. Establishment of pm office?

7. Do you know the roles & responsibilities required for this Organizational Infrastructure project?

8. When must it be done?

9. Does it make any difference if you am successful?

10. Just how important is your work to the overall success of the Organizational Infrastructure project?

11. Were escalated issues resolved promptly?

12. How well did the chosen processes produce the expected results?

13. Mitigate. what will you do to minimize the impact

should the risk event occur?

14. What do they need to know about the Organizational Infrastructure project?

15. What will you do to minimize the impact should a risk event occur?

16. Were decisions made in a timely manner?

17. How should needs be met?

18. At which cmmi level are software processes documented, standardized, and integrated into a standard to-be practiced process for your organization?

19. If the risk event occurs, what will you do?

20. What must be done?

1.1 Project Charter: Organizational Infrastructure

21. Why use a Organizational Infrastructure project charter?

22. How will you know that a change is an improvement?

23. Why do you manage integration?

24. Why Outsource?

25. Why is a Organizational Infrastructure project Charter used?

26. What does it need to do?

27. Why do you need to manage scope?

28. For whom?

29. How will you learn more about the process or system you are trying to improve?

30. How high should you set your goals?

31. Organizational Infrastructure project deliverables: what is the Organizational Infrastructure project going to produce?

32. What are you striving to accomplish (measurable goal(s))?

33. What is the business need?

34. Is it an improvement over existing products?

35. What is in it for you?

36. What are the known stakeholder requirements?

37. What are the assigned resources?

38. What is the purpose of the Organizational Infrastructure project?

39. What material?

1.2 Stakeholder Register: Organizational Infrastructure

40. What is the power of the stakeholder?

41. How should employers make voices heard?

42. What & Why?

43. What are the major Organizational Infrastructure project milestones requiring communications or providing communications opportunities?

44. Who is managing stakeholder engagement?

45. How much influence do they have on the Organizational Infrastructure project?

46. Who wants to talk about Security?

47. Who are the stakeholders?

48. Is your organization ready for change?

49. How big is the gap?

50. How will reports be created?

51. What opportunities exist to provide communications?

1.3 Stakeholder Analysis Matrix: Organizational Infrastructure

52. How will the Organizational Infrastructure project benefit them?

53. Is there evidence that demonstrates the impact of education on the Organizational Infrastructure projects outcomes?

54. Who will promote/support the Organizational Infrastructure project, provided that they are involved?

55. How are you predicting what future (work)loads will be?

56. What do you need to appraise?

57. How can you counter negative efforts?

58. Are they likely to influence the success or failure of your Organizational Infrastructure project?

59. Who is most dependent on the resources at stake?

60. Niche target markets?

61. Why is it important to identify them?

62. How to measure the achievement of the Immediate Objective?

63. What advantages do your organizations stakeholders have?

64. If the baseline is now, and if its improved it will be better than now?

65. Is changing technology threatening your organizations position?

66. Who is directly responsible for decisions on issues important to the Organizational Infrastructure project?

67. What are innovative aspects of your organization?

68. Information and research?

69. Which conditions out of the control of the management are crucial to contribute for the achievement of the development objective?

70. Innovative aspects?

71. Opponents; who are the opponents?

2.0 Planning Process Group: Organizational Infrastructure

72. Does it make any difference if you are successful?

73. How are it Organizational Infrastructure projects different?

74. If a task is partitionable, is this a sufficient condition to reduce the Organizational Infrastructure project duration?

75. How does activity resource estimation affect activity duration estimation?

76. What factors are contributing to progress or delay in the achievement of products and results?

77. How will it affect you?

78. Why is it important to determine activity sequencing on Organizational Infrastructure projects?

79. To what extent and in what ways are the Organizational Infrastructure project contributing to progress towards organizational reform?

80. When will the Organizational Infrastructure project be done?

81. In what ways can the governance of the Organizational Infrastructure project be improved so that it has greater likelihood of achieving future

sustainability?

82. What will you do?

83. In what way has the program contributed towards the issue culture and development included on the public agenda?

84. Do the partners have sufficient financial capacity to keep up the benefits produced by the programme?

85. The Organizational Infrastructure project charter is created in which Organizational Infrastructure project management process group?

86. If a risk event occurs, what will you do?

87. How well did the chosen processes fit the needs of the Organizational Infrastructure project?

88. What do you need to do?

89. To what extent do the intervention objectives and strategies of the Organizational Infrastructure project respond to your organizations plans?

90. Who are the Organizational Infrastructure project stakeholders?

91. Are the necessary foundations in place to ensure the sustainability of the results of the Organizational Infrastructure project?

2.1 Project Management Plan: Organizational Infrastructure

92. Are cost risk analysis methods applied to develop contingencies for the estimated total Organizational Infrastructure project costs?

93. Who is the sponsor?

94. What are the assumptions?

95. Was the peer (technical) review of the cost estimates duly coordinated with the cost estimate center of expertise and addressed in the review documentation and certification?

96. Are there any client staffing expectations?

97. What went right?

98. What if, for example, the positive direction and vision of your organization causes expected trends to change resulting in greater need than expected?

99. Are the proposed Organizational Infrastructure project purposes different than a previously authorized Organizational Infrastructure project?

100. Who is the Organizational Infrastructure project Manager?

101. Will you add a schedule and diagram?

102. What should you drop in order to add something new?

103. Are comparable cost estimates used for comparing, screening and selecting alternative plans, and has a reasonable cost estimate been developed for the recommended plan?

104. Is the appropriate plan selected based on your organizations objectives and evaluation criteria expressed in Principles and Guidelines policies?

105. Is there an incremental analysis/cost effectiveness analysis of proposed mitigation features based on an approved method and using an accepted model?

106. What goes into your Organizational Infrastructure project Charter?

107. Are calculations and results of analyzes essentially correct?

108. What are the training needs?

109. When is a Organizational Infrastructure project management plan created?

110. Does the implementation plan have an appropriate division of responsibilities?

2.2 Scope Management Plan: Organizational Infrastructure

111. Have all necessary approvals been obtained?

112. Product – what are you trying to accomplish and how will you know when you are finished?

113. Would the Organizational Infrastructure project cost sharing involve reimbursement to the sponsor?

114. What weaknesses do you have?

115. Are all payments made according to the contract(s)?

116. Are you doing what you have set out to do?

117. Has a provision been made to reassess Organizational Infrastructure project risks at various Organizational Infrastructure project stages?

118. Timeline and milestones?

119. Is there an issues management plan in place?

120. Are metrics used to evaluate and manage Vendors?

121. Are the Organizational Infrastructure project plans updated on a frequent basis?

122. When will scope verification be performed?

123. Does the detailed work plan match the complexity of tasks with the capabilities of personnel?

124. Is there a scope management plan that includes how Organizational Infrastructure project scope will be defined, developed, monitored, validated and controlled?

125. Are the payment terms being followed?

126. Knowing the health of the Organizational Infrastructure project – What is the status?

127. Are written status reports provided on a designated frequent basis?

128. Are the people assigned to the Organizational Infrastructure project sufficiently qualified?

2.3 Requirements Management Plan: Organizational Infrastructure

129. How will the requirements become prioritized?

130. Who will perform the analysis?

131. What is a problem?

132. Will you have access to stakeholders when you need them?

133. What went wrong?

134. Is the user satisfied?

135. Do you know which stakeholders will participate in the requirements effort?

136. Has the requirements team been instructed in the Change Control process?

137. Did you distinguish the scope of work the contractor(s) will be required to do?

138. Did you get proper approvals?

139. Will you perform a Requirements Risk assessment and develop a plan to deal with risks?

140. What information regarding the Organizational Infrastructure project requirements will be reported?

141. What is the earliest finish date for this Organizational Infrastructure project if it is scheduled to start on ...?

142. Will the product release be stable and mature enough to be deployed in the user community?

143. What performance metrics will be used?

144. Will the Organizational Infrastructure project requirements become approved in writing?

145. Do you expect stakeholders to be cooperative?

146. Is stakeholder risk tolerance an important factor for the requirements process in this Organizational Infrastructure project?

147. Will the contractors involved take full responsibility?

148. How will the information be distributed?

2.4 Requirements Documentation: Organizational Infrastructure

149. What will be the integration problems?

150. What variations exist for a process?

151. How does what is being described meet the business need?

152. Is the requirement properly understood?

153. What are current process problems?

154. What is the risk associated with the technology?

155. What is effective documentation?

156. Is new technology needed?

157. Who provides requirements?

158. Is the origin of the requirement clearly stated?

159. What are the potential disadvantages/ advantages?

160. What is the risk associated with cost and schedule?

161. Basic work/business process; high-level, what is being touched?

162. Consistency. are there any requirements conflicts?

163. Who is interacting with the system?

164. Verifiability. can the requirements be checked?

165. Who is involved?

166. What images does it conjure?

167. Can the requirements be checked?

168. Where do system and software requirements come from, what are sources?

2.5 Requirements Traceability Matrix: Organizational Infrastructure

169. Will you use a Requirements Traceability Matrix?

170. What are the chronologies, contingencies, consequences, criteria?

171. What is the WBS?

172. How do you manage scope?

173. Why do you manage scope?

174. How will it affect the stakeholders personally in career?

175. Is there a requirements traceability process in place?

176. Describe the process for approving requirements so they can be added to the traceability matrix and Organizational Infrastructure project work can be performed. Will the Organizational Infrastructure project requirements become approved in writing?

177. How small is small enough?

178. Do you have a clear understanding of all subcontracts in place?

179. Why use a WBS?

180. What percentage of Organizational Infrastructure projects are producing traceability matrices between requirements and other work products?

2.6 Project Scope Statement: Organizational Infrastructure

181. Elements that deal with providing the detail?

182. Risks?

183. Is an issue management process documented and filed?

184. Have you been able to thoroughly document the Organizational Infrastructure projects assumptions and constraints?

185. Were potential customers involved early in the planning process?

186. What is a process you might recommend to verify the accuracy of the research deliverable?

187. Change management vs. change leadership - what is the difference?

188. Write a brief purpose statement for this Organizational Infrastructure project. Include a business justification statement. What is the product of this Organizational Infrastructure project?

189. Any new risks introduced or old risks impacted. Are there issues that could affect the existing requirements for the result, service, or product if the scope changes?

190. Where and how does the team fit within your organization structure?

191. Is the plan under configuration management?

192. What process would you recommend for creating the Organizational Infrastructure project scope statement?

193. Will the risk status be reported to management on a regular and frequent basis?

194. Has the Organizational Infrastructure project scope statement been reviewed as part of the baseline process?

195. Are there completion/verification criteria defined for each task producing an output?

2.7 Assumption and Constraint Log: Organizational Infrastructure

196. After observing execution of process, is it in compliance with the documented Plan?

197. How relevant is this attribute to this Organizational Infrastructure project or audit?

198. Have all involved stakeholders and work groups committed to the Organizational Infrastructure project?

199. Can the requirements be traced to the appropriate components of the solution, as well as test scripts?

200. Is the amount of effort justified by the anticipated value of forming a new process?

201. Are there processes defining how software will be developed including development methods, overall timeline for development, software product standards, and traceability?

202. Is the process working, and people are not executing in compliance of the process?

203. What other teams / processes would be impacted by changes to the current process, and how?

204. Are funding and staffing resource estimates sufficiently detailed and documented for use

in planning and tracking the Organizational Infrastructure project?

205. What does an audit system look like?

206. No superfluous information or marketing narrative?

207. Were the system requirements formally reviewed prior to initiating the design phase?

208. Are there ways to reduce the time it takes to get something approved?

209. Have Organizational Infrastructure project management standards and procedures been established and documented?

210. What strengths do you have?

211. Are there processes in place to ensure that all the terms and code concepts have been documented consistently?

212. Does the document/deliverable meet all requirements (for example, statement of work) specific to this deliverable?

213. Are processes for release management of new development from coding and unit testing, to integration testing, to training, and production defined and followed?

214. Are there unnecessary steps that are creating bottlenecks and/or causing people to wait?

2.8 Work Breakdown Structure: Organizational Infrastructure

215. How many levels?

216. What is the probability that the Organizational Infrastructure project duration will exceed xx weeks?

217. When do you stop?

218. When does it have to be done?

219. How will you and your Organizational Infrastructure project team define the Organizational Infrastructure projects scope and work breakdown structure?

220. What is the probability of completing the Organizational Infrastructure project in less that xx days?

221. Where does it take place?

222. Who has to do it?

223. Why would you develop a Work Breakdown Structure?

224. Why is it useful?

225. Can you make it?

226. Is it still viable?

227. How big is a work-package?

228. When would you develop a Work Breakdown Structure?

229. How much detail?

230. Is the work breakdown structure (wbs) defined and is the scope of the Organizational Infrastructure project clear with assigned deliverable owners?

231. Is it a change in scope?

2.9 WBS Dictionary: Organizational Infrastructure

232. Do work packages consist of discrete tasks which are adequately described?

233. Are the overhead pools formally and adequately identified?

234. Are budgets or values assigned to work packages and planning packages in terms of dollars, hours, or other measurable units?

235. Budgets assigned to major functional organizations?

236. Does the contractor require sufficient detailed planning of control accounts to constrain the application of budget initially allocated for future effort to current effort?

237. Incurrence of actual indirect costs in excess of budgets, by element of expense?

238. Are estimates of costs at completion generated in a rational, consistent manner?

239. Are work packages reasonably short in time duration or do they have adequate objective indicators/milestones to minimize subjectivity of the in process work evaluation?

240. Are estimates of costs at completion utilized

in determining contract funding requirements and reporting them?

241. Are retroactive changes to BCWS and BCWP prohibited except for correction of errors or for normal accounting adjustments?

242. Performance to date and material commitment?

243. Should you include sub-activities?

244. Are work packages assigned to performing organizations?

245. Changes in the direct base to which overhead costs are allocated?

246. Is the anticipated (firm and potential) business base Organizational Infrastructure projected in a rational, consistent manner?

247. Are estimates developed by Organizational Infrastructure project personnel coordinated with the already stated responsible for overall management to determine whether required resources will be available according to revised planning?

248. Are the latest revised estimates of costs at completion compared with the established budgets at appropriate levels and causes of variances identified?

249. Are material costs reported within the same period as that in which BCWP is earned for that material?

250. Are current budgets resulting from changes to the authorized work and/or internal replanning, reconcilable to original budgets for specified reporting items?

2.10 Schedule Management Plan: Organizational Infrastructure

251. Is an industry recognized mechanized support tool(s) being used for Organizational Infrastructure project scheduling & tracking?

252. Are decisions captured in a decisions log?

253. Are enough systems & user personnel assigned to the Organizational Infrastructure project?

254. Must the Organizational Infrastructure project be complete by a specified date?

255. Have Organizational Infrastructure project success criteria been defined?

256. Has a sponsor been identified?

257. Are the key elements of a Organizational Infrastructure project Charter present?

258. Why conduct schedule analysis?

259. Are assumptions being identified, recorded, analyzed, qualified and closed?

260. Are updated Organizational Infrastructure project time & resource estimates reasonable based on the current Organizational Infrastructure project stage?

261. Are changes in deliverable commitments agreed to by all affected groups & individuals?

262. Are actuals compared against estimates to analyze and correct variances?

263. Are software metrics formally captured, analyzed and used as a basis for other Organizational Infrastructure project estimates?

264. Are vendor contract reports, reviews and visits conducted periodically?

265. Is your organization certified as a broker of the products/supplies?

266. Is the schedule feasible and at what cost?

267. Are the activity durations realistic and at an appropriate level of detail for effective management?

268. Is there a formal set of procedures supporting Stakeholder Management?

2.11 Activity List: Organizational Infrastructure

269. How should ongoing costs be monitored to try to keep the Organizational Infrastructure project within budget?

270. What is the probability the Organizational Infrastructure project can be completed in xx weeks?

271. What are you counting on?

272. What is the total time required to complete the Organizational Infrastructure project if no delays occur?

273. For other activities, how much delay can be tolerated?

274. Who will perform the work?

275. Are the required resources available or need to be acquired?

276. When will the work be performed?

277. When do the individual activities need to start and finish?

278. What went well?

279. What is your organizations history in doing similar activities?

280. What will be performed?

281. Can you determine the activity that must finish, before this activity can start?

282. Where will it be performed?

283. What is the LF and LS for each activity?

284. How do you determine the late start (LS) for each activity?

285. The wbs is developed as part of a joint planning session. and how do you know that youhave done this right?

286. How much slack is available in the Organizational Infrastructure project?

2.12 Activity Attributes: Organizational Infrastructure

287. Time for overtime?

288. Can more resources be added?

289. How do you manage time?

290. Why?

291. Is there a trend during the year?

292. Activity: fair or not fair?

293. What is the general pattern here?

294. How many days do you need to complete the work scope with a limit of X number of resources?

295. Do you feel very comfortable with your prediction?

296. Activity: what is In the Bag?

297. Where else does it apply?

298. What is missing?

299. What activity do you think you should spend the most time on?

300. Does your organization of the data change its

meaning?

301. Have constraints been applied to the start and finish milestones for the phases?

302. How many resources do you need to complete the work scope within a limit of X number of days?

2.13 Milestone List: Organizational Infrastructure

303. Continuity, supply chain robustness?

304. What has been done so far?

305. What date will the task finish?

306. It is to be a narrative text providing the crucial aspects of your Organizational Infrastructure project proposal answering what, who, how, when and where?

307. How will the milestone be verified?

308. Loss of key staff?

309. Global influences?

310. How will you get the word out to customers?

311. Timescales, deadlines and pressures?

312. Competitive advantages?

313. Identify critical paths (one or more) and which activities are on the critical path?

314. Vital contracts and partners?

315. What are your competitors vulnerabilities?

316. Obstacles faced?

317. How difficult will it be to do specific activities on this Organizational Infrastructure project?

318. How late can the activity start?

319. Reliability of data, plan predictability?

2.14 Network Diagram: Organizational Infrastructure

320. What is the probability of completing the Organizational Infrastructure project in less that xx days?

321. Planning: who, how long, what to do?

322. How confident can you be in your milestone dates and the delivery date?

323. What job or jobs precede it?

324. Are the gantt chart and/or network diagram updated periodically and used to assess the overall Organizational Infrastructure project timetable?

325. What to do and When?

326. Review the logical flow of the network diagram. Take a look at which activities you have first and then sequence the activities. Do they make sense?

327. What are the Major Administrative Issues?

328. How difficult will it be to do specific activities on this Organizational Infrastructure project?

329. What job or jobs follow it?

330. What controls the start and finish of a job?

331. Are you on time?

332. What activities must follow this activity?

333. What are the tools?

334. What activities must occur simultaneously with this activity?

335. What is the completion time?

336. What must be completed before an activity can be started?

337. What can be done concurrently?

338. What is the lowest cost to complete this Organizational Infrastructure project in xx weeks?

2.15 Activity Resource Requirements: Organizational Infrastructure

339. Other support in specific areas?

340. Do you use tools like decomposition and rolling-wave planning to produce the activity list and other outputs?

341. How many signatures do you require on a check and does this match what is in your policy and procedures?

342. Organizational Applicability?

343. Are there unresolved issues that need to be addressed?

344. Why do you do that?

345. How do you handle petty cash?

346. Which logical relationship does the PDM use most often?

347. What is the Work Plan Standard?

348. What are constraints that you might find during the Human Resource Planning process?

349. Is there anything planned that does not need to be here?

350. Anything else?

351. When does monitoring begin?

2.16 Resource Breakdown Structure: Organizational Infrastructure

352. Who will use the system?

353. When do they need the information?

354. How can this help you with team building?

355. What is the purpose of assigning and documenting responsibility?

356. How difficult will it be to do specific activities on this Organizational Infrastructure project?

357. Why is this important?

358. Changes based on input from stakeholders?

359. Who needs what information?

360. What is Organizational Infrastructure project communication management?

361. Who is allowed to see what data about which resources?

362. What is the primary purpose of the human resource plan?

363. Why do you do it?

364. What is each stakeholders desired outcome for

the Organizational Infrastructure project?

365. What are the requirements for resource data?

366. What can you do to improve productivity?

367. How should the information be delivered?

2.17 Activity Duration Estimates: Organizational Infrastructure

368. How can others help Organizational Infrastructure project managers understand your organizational context for Organizational Infrastructure projects?

369. Are performance reviews conducted regularly to assess the status of Organizational Infrastructure projects?

370. How could you define throughput and how would your organization benefit from maximizing it?

371. Briefly summarize the work done by Maslow, Herzberg, McClellan, McGregor, Ouchi, Thamhain and Wilemon, and Covey. How do theories relate to Organizational Infrastructure project management?

372. Briefly describe some key events in the history of Organizational Infrastructure project management. What Organizational Infrastructure project was the first to use modern Organizational Infrastructure project management?

373. How does the job market and current state of the economy affect human resource management?

374. Are Organizational Infrastructure project management tools and techniques consistently applied throughout all Organizational Infrastructure projects?

375. Why is outsourcing growing so rapidly?

376. What type of contract was used and why?

377. Consider the changes in the job market for information technology workers. How does the job market and current state of the economy affect human resource management?

378. Which types of reports would help provide summary information to senior management?

379. Does a process exist to identify which qualified resources may be attainable?

380. Do you think Organizational Infrastructure project managers of large information technology Organizational Infrastructure projects need strong technical skills?

381. Account for the make-or-buy process and how to perform the financial calculations involved in the process. What are the main types of contracts if you do decide to outsource?

382. Are Organizational Infrastructure project activities decomposed into manageable components to ensure expected management control?

383. Is risk identification completed regularly throughout the Organizational Infrastructure project?

384. Could it have been avoided?

385. Why should Organizational Infrastructure project

managers strive to make jobs look easy?

386. Are the causes of all variances identified?

2.18 Duration Estimating Worksheet: Organizational Infrastructure

387. Do any colleagues have experience with your organization and/or RFPs?

388. What is cost and Organizational Infrastructure project cost management?

389. When, then?

390. Is this operation cost effective?

391. How can the Organizational Infrastructure project be displayed graphically to better visualize the activities?

392. Will the Organizational Infrastructure project collaborate with the local community and leverage resources?

393. What work will be included in the Organizational Infrastructure project?

394. When does your organization expect to be able to complete it?

395. What info is needed?

396. Small or large Organizational Infrastructure project?

397. Is a construction detail attached (to aid in

explanation)?

398. Why estimate time and cost?

399. How should ongoing costs be monitored to try to keep the Organizational Infrastructure project within budget?

400. What is the total time required to complete the Organizational Infrastructure project if no delays occur?

401. What utility impacts are there?

402. Is the Organizational Infrastructure project responsive to community need?

403. Science = process: remember the scientific method?

2.19 Project Schedule: Organizational Infrastructure

404. Master Organizational Infrastructure project schedule?

405. How can you fix it?

406. To what degree is do you feel the entire team was committed to the Organizational Infrastructure project schedule?

407. Is the structure for tracking the Organizational Infrastructure project schedule well defined and assigned to a specific individual?

408. How do you use schedules?

409. What documents, if any, will the subcontractor provide (eg Organizational Infrastructure project schedule, quality plan etc)?

410. What is Organizational Infrastructure project management?

411. How can you address that situation?

412. Did the Organizational Infrastructure project come in on schedule?

413. How detailed should a Organizational Infrastructure project get?

414. Activity charts and bar charts are graphical representations of a Organizational Infrastructure project schedule ...how do they differ?

415. Why do you need schedules?

416. Understand the constraints used in preparing the schedule. Are activities connected because logic dictates the order in which others occur?

417. Why do you need to manage Organizational Infrastructure project Risk?

418. Are there activities that came from a template or previous Organizational Infrastructure project that are not applicable on this phase of this Organizational Infrastructure project?

419. Is the Organizational Infrastructure project schedule available for all Organizational Infrastructure project team members to review?

420. How closely did the initial Organizational Infrastructure project Schedule compare with the actual schedule?

421. Change management required?

422. How do you know that youhave done this right?

2.20 Cost Management Plan: Organizational Infrastructure

423. Have the key functions and capabilities been defined and assigned to each release or iteration?

424. How does the proposed individual meet each requirement?

425. Were stakeholders aware and supportive of the principles and practices of modern software estimation?

426. Are the Organizational Infrastructure project plans updated on a frequent basis?

427. Are the appropriate IT resources adequate to meet planned commitments?

428. Does a documented Organizational Infrastructure project organizational policy & plan (i.e. governance model) exist?

429. Personnel with expertise?

430. Has the budget been baselined?

431. Are vendor invoices audited for accuracy before payment?

432. Was the scope definition used in task sequencing?

433. Vac -variance at completion, how much over/ under budget do you expect to be?

434. Are software metrics formally captured, analyzed and used as a basis for other Organizational Infrastructure project estimates?

435. Are the Organizational Infrastructure project team members located locally to the users/ stakeholders?

436. Is quality monitored from the perspective of the customers needs and expectations?

437. Is a payment system in place with proper reviews and approvals?

438. Quality assurance overheads?

439. Has the Organizational Infrastructure project manager been identified?

440. Sensitivity analysis?

441. Estimating responsibilities – how will the responsibilities for cost estimating be allocated?

2.21 Activity Cost Estimates: Organizational Infrastructure

442. What is the activity inventory?

443. Why do you manage cost?

444. What cost data should be used to estimate costs during the 2-year follow-up period?

445. How do you change activities?

446. When do you enter into PPM?

447. What is the activity recast of the budget?

448. How do you treat administrative costs in the activity inventory?

449. Are cost subtotals needed?

450. Where can you get activity reports?

451. Was it performed on time?

452. What communication items need improvement?

453. What were things that you did very well and want to do the same again on the next Organizational Infrastructure project?

454. What do you want to know about the stay to know if costs were inappropriately high or low?

455. Measurable - are the targets measurable?

456. What were things that you did well, and could improve, and how?

457. Certification of actual expenditures?

458. What areas does the group agree are the biggest success on the Organizational Infrastructure project?

459. What are you looking for?

2.22 Cost Estimating Worksheet: Organizational Infrastructure

460. What additional Organizational Infrastructure project(s) could be initiated as a result of this Organizational Infrastructure project?

461. Is it feasible to establish a control group arrangement?

462. Ask: are others positioned to know, are others credible, and will others cooperate?

463. What costs are to be estimated?

464. Is the Organizational Infrastructure project responsive to community need?

465. What is the estimated labor cost today based upon this information?

466. What is the purpose of estimating?

467. What can be included?

468. Value pocket identification & quantification what are value pockets?

469. Does the Organizational Infrastructure project provide innovative ways for stakeholders to overcome obstacles or deliver better outcomes?

470. Will the Organizational Infrastructure project

collaborate with the local community and leverage resources?

471. Who is best positioned to know and assist in identifying corresponding factors?

472. How will the results be shared and to whom?

473. What happens to any remaining funds not used?

474. Can a trend be established from historical performance data on the selected measure and are the criteria for using trend analysis or forecasting methods met?

475. Identify the timeframe necessary to monitor progress and collect data to determine how the selected measure has changed?

476. What will others want?

2.23 Cost Baseline: Organizational Infrastructure

477. How will cost estimates be used?

478. Definition of done can be traced back to the definitions of what are you providing to the customer in terms of deliverables?

479. What would the life cycle costs be?

480. Is there anything you need from upper management in order to be successful?

481. How do you manage cost?

482. Does it impact schedule, cost, quality?

483. How long are you willing to wait before you find out were late?

484. What does a good WBS NOT look like?

485. What deliverables come first?

486. What do you want to measure ?

487. Have you identified skills that are missing from your team?

488. Does the suggested change request represent a desired enhancement to the products functionality?

489. Have all approved changes to the Organizational Infrastructure project requirement been identified and impact on the performance, cost, and schedule baselines documented?

490. What is your organizations history in doing similar tasks?

491. Have the lessons learned been filed with the Organizational Infrastructure project Management Office?

492. Has the documentation relating to operation and maintenance of the product(s) or service(s) been delivered to, and accepted by, operations management?

493. What threats might prevent you from getting there?

494. Has operations management formally accepted responsibility for operating and maintaining the product(s) or service(s) delivered by the Organizational Infrastructure project?

495. Has the Organizational Infrastructure project (or Organizational Infrastructure project phase) been evaluated against each objective established in the product description and Integrated Organizational Infrastructure project Plan?

2.24 Quality Management Plan: Organizational Infrastructure

496. What are you trying to accomplish?

497. You know what your customers expectations are regarding this process?

498. List your organizations customer contact standards that employees are expected to maintain. How are corresponding standards measured?

499. How are corresponding standards measured?

500. Does the program use modeling in the permitting or decision-making processes?

501. How do you field-modify testing procedures?

502. How do you decide what information to record?

503. Do you periodically review your data quality system to see that it is up to date and appropriate?

504. Are formal code reviews conducted?

505. Results Available?

506. Checking the completeness and appropriateness of the sampling and testing. Were the right locations/samples tested for the right parameters?

507. What are your key performance measures/

indicators for tracking progress relative to your action plans?

508. How are training records kept?

509. What are the appropriate test methods to be used?

510. How relevant is this attribute to this Organizational Infrastructure project or audit?

511. How are senior leaders, employees, and your organization involved in supporting the community?

512. How effectively was the Quality Management Plan applied during Organizational Infrastructure project Execution?

513. How are changes to procedures made?

514. Modifications to the requirements?

2.25 Quality Metrics: Organizational Infrastructure

515. How are requirements conflicts resolved?

516. Has risk analysis been adequately reviewed?

517. Do you know how much profit a 10% decrease in waste would generate?

518. Was review conducted per standard protocols?

519. What if the biggest risk to your business were the already stated people who do not complain?

520. When will the Final Guidance will be issued?

521. Why is now the time for quality metrics?

522. What method of measurement do you use?

523. Where did complaints, returns and warranty claims come from?

524. How do you communicate results and findings to upper management?

525. What is the CMS Benchmark?

526. Who notifies stakeholders of normal and abnormal results?

527. What forces exist that would cause them to

change?

528. Did evaluation start on time?

529. How should customers provide input?

530. What level of statistical confidence do you use?

531. Is there alignment within your organization on definitions?

532. Product Availability ?

533. How do you calculate such metrics?

534. Which data do others need in one place to target areas of improvement?

2.26 Process Improvement Plan: Organizational Infrastructure

535. Have the frequency of collection and the points in the process where measurements will be made been determined?

536. Are you making progress on your improvement plan?

537. Does your process ensure quality?

538. What actions are needed to address the problems and achieve the goals?

539. Why do you want to achieve the goal?

540. Are you following the quality standards?

541. What personnel are the change agents for your initiative?

542. Who should prepare the process improvement action plan?

543. What makes people good SPI coaches?

544. Management commitment at all levels?

545. Where are you now?

546. What lessons have you learned so far?

547. Where do you want to be?

548. Modeling current processes is great, and will you ever see a return on that investment?

549. The motive is determined by asking, Why do you want to achieve this goal?

550. Are you meeting the quality standards?

551. How do you measure?

552. Everyone agrees on what process improvement is, right?

2.27 Responsibility Assignment Matrix: Organizational Infrastructure

553. Do you know how your people are allocated?

554. Identify potential or actual budget-based and time-based schedule variances?

555. Which Organizational Infrastructure project management knowledge area is least mature?

556. How do you manage human resources?

557. Are others working on the right things?

558. Is work progressively subdivided into detailed work packages as requirements are defined?

559. What cost control tool do many experts say is crucial to Organizational Infrastructure project management?

560. Evaluate the impact of schedule changes, work around, etc?

561. What do you do when people do not respond?

562. What tool can show you individual and group allocations?

563. The staff characteristics – is the group or the person capable to work together as a team?

564. When performing is split among two or more roles, is the work clearly defined so that the efforts are coordinated and the communication is clear?

565. Are detailed work packages planned as far in advance as practicable?

566. Are overhead cost budgets established for each organization which has authority to incur overhead costs?

567. Are data elements reconcilable between internal summary reports and reports forwarded to stakeholders?

2.28 Roles and Responsibilities: Organizational Infrastructure

568. What expectations were NOT met?

569. What specific behaviors did you observe?

570. Do the values and practices inherent in the culture of your organization foster or hinder the process?

571. Does your vision/mission support a culture of quality data?

572. Accountabilities: what are the roles and responsibilities of individual team members?

573. How is your work-life balance?

574. Implementation of actions: Who are the responsible units?

575. How well did the Organizational Infrastructure project Team understand the expectations of specific roles and responsibilities?

576. Who: who is involved?

577. Who is responsible for implementation activities and where will the functions, roles and responsibilities be defined?

578. Are your budgets supportive of a culture of

quality data?

579. Are governance roles and responsibilities documented?

580. What areas would you highlight for changes or improvements?

581. Do you take the time to clearly define roles and responsibilities on Organizational Infrastructure project tasks?

582. Was the expectation clearly communicated?

583. Are Organizational Infrastructure project team roles and responsibilities identified and documented?

584. Required skills, knowledge, experience?

585. What expectations were met?

2.29 Human Resource Management Plan: Organizational Infrastructure

586. Is Organizational Infrastructure project work proceeding in accordance with the original Organizational Infrastructure project schedule?

587. Is there a Quality Management Plan?

588. Are there checklists created to determine if all quality processes are followed?

589. Is a stakeholder management plan in place that covers topics?

590. Is the current culture aligned with the vision, mission, and values of the department?

591. Are adequate resources provided for the quality assurance function?

592. Identify who is needed on the core Organizational Infrastructure project team to complete Organizational Infrastructure project deliverables and achieve its goals and objectives. What skills, knowledge and experiences are required?

593. Was your organizations estimating methodology being used and followed?

594. What areas were overlooked on this Organizational Infrastructure project?

595. Does the schedule include Organizational Infrastructure project management time and change request analysis time?

596. How to convince to employees that it is a necessary process?

597. How relevant is this attribute to this Organizational Infrastructure project or audit?

598. Is there general agreement & acceptance of the current status and progress of the Organizational Infrastructure project?

599. Are change requests logged and managed?

600. Are action items captured and managed?

601. Has your organization readiness assessment been conducted?

602. How to convince employees that this is a necessary process?

2.30 Communications Management Plan: Organizational Infrastructure

603. What data is going to be required?

604. Who to learn from?

605. Are there potential barriers between the team and the stakeholder?

606. What is the stakeholders level of authority?

607. Who is the stakeholder?

608. Are you constantly rushing from meeting to meeting?

609. Who did you turn to if you had questions?

610. Who have you worked with in past, similar initiatives?

611. Are there too many who have an interest in some aspect of your work?

612. Who is responsible?

613. What help do you and your team need from the stakeholder?

614. Why do you manage communications?

615. Which team member will work with each

stakeholder?

616. What steps can you take for a positive relationship?

617. Who to share with?

618. Why is stakeholder engagement important?

619. How is this initiative related to other portfolios, programs, or Organizational Infrastructure projects?

620. Timing: when do the effects of the communication take place?

621. What are the interrelationships?

622. Which stakeholders can influence others?

2.31 Risk Management Plan: Organizational Infrastructure

623. Do benefits and chances of success outweigh potential damage if success is not attained?

624. Are the reports useful and easy to read?

625. People risk -are people with appropriate skills available to help complete the Organizational Infrastructure project?

626. What risks are tracked?

627. Are the participants able to keep up with the workload?

628. Is there anything you would now do differently on your Organizational Infrastructure project based on this experience?

629. How well were you able to manage your risk before?

630. Has something like this been done before?

631. Which is an input to the risk management process?

632. Which risks should get the attention?

633. Risk probability and impact: how will the probabilities and impacts of risk items be assessed?

634. Should the risk be taken at all?

635. Havent software Organizational Infrastructure projects been late before?

636. What will drive change?

637. Are tool mentors available?

638. What other risks are created by choosing an avoidance strategy?

639. Are people attending meetings and doing work?

640. Are the metrics meaningful and useful?

641. Do requirements put excessive performance constraints on the product?

2.32 Risk Register: Organizational Infrastructure

642. Budget and schedule: what are the estimated costs and schedules for performing risk-related activities?

643. What may happen or not go according to plan?

644. Can the likelihood and impact of failing to achieve corresponding recommendations and action plans be assessed?

645. How often will the Risk Management Plan and Risk Register be formally reviewed, and by whom?

646. Does the evidence highlight any areas to advance opportunities or foster good relations. If yes what steps will be taken?

647. Do you require further engagement?

648. How well are risks controlled?

649. Who needs to know about this?

650. Methodology: how will risk management be performed on this Organizational Infrastructure project?

651. What are you going to do to limit the Organizational Infrastructure projects risk exposure due to the identified risks?

652. When would you develop a risk register?

653. What evidence do you have to justify the likelihood score of the risk (audit, incident report, claim, complaints, inspection, internal review)?

654. What should the audit role be in establishing a risk management process?

655. Having taken action, how did the responses effect change, and where is the Organizational Infrastructure project now?

656. What is a Risk?

657. Manageability – have mitigations to the risk been identified?

658. When will it happen?

659. Who is going to do it?

2.33 Probability and Impact Assessment: Organizational Infrastructure

660. What are the chances the event will occur?

661. What risks are necessary to achieve success?

662. Who will be in command to monitor and control the performance of the consortium members (consortium leader/client)?

663. Has the need for the Organizational Infrastructure project been properly established?

664. Who should be responsible for the monitoring and tracking of the indicators youhave identified?

665. Can the Organizational Infrastructure project proceed without assuming the risk?

666. How completely has the customer been identified?

667. How realistic is the timing of introduction?

668. Can you stabilize dynamic risk factors?

669. What is the risk appetite?

670. How will economic events and trends likely affect the Organizational Infrastructure project?

671. What should be the level of difficulty in handling the technology?

672. Is the number of people on the Organizational Infrastructure project team adequate to do the job?

673. Are the risk data timely and relevant?

674. What should be the level of coordination?

675. Does the software engineering team have the right mix of skills?

676. Is the Organizational Infrastructure project cutting across the entire organization?

677. Have you worked with the customer in the past?

678. Would avoiding any of corresponding impact the Organizational Infrastructure projects chance of success?

679. Monitoring of the overall Organizational Infrastructure project status – are there any changes in the Organizational Infrastructure project that can effect and cause new possible risks?

2.34 Probability and Impact Matrix: Organizational Infrastructure

680. During Organizational Infrastructure project executing, a major problem occurs that was not included in the risk register. What should you do FIRST?

681. How do you analyze the risks in the different types of Organizational Infrastructure projects?

682. Have top software and customer managers formally committed to support the Organizational Infrastructure project?

683. Do you need a risk management plan?

684. How to prioritize risks?

685. During which risk management process is a determination to transfer a risk made?

686. Have staff received necessary training?

687. What are its business ethics?

688. Risk may be made during which step of risk management?

689. What are the levels of understanding of the future users of this technology?

690. Which phase of the Organizational Infrastructure

project do you take part in?

691. Who is going to be the consortium leader?

692. Economic to take on the Organizational Infrastructure project?

693. How would you suggest monitoring for risk transition indicators?

694. What would be the effect of slippage?

695. What is the industrial relations prevailing in this organization?

696. Have customers been involved fully in the definition of requirements?

2.35 Risk Data Sheet: Organizational Infrastructure

697. Type of risk identified?

698. What if client refuses?

699. What are the main threats to your existence?

700. How do you handle product safely?

701. Potential for recurrence?

702. Whom do you serve (customers)?

703. Who has a vested interest in how you perform as your organization (our stakeholders)?

704. Risk of what?

705. Do effective diagnostic tests exist?

706. What is the chance that it will happen?

707. What are you trying to achieve (Objectives)?

708. What are the main opportunities available to you that you should grab while you can?

709. If it happens, what are the consequences?

710. Has a sensitivity analysis been carried out?

711. Are new hazards created?

712. Is the data sufficiently specified in terms of the type of failure being analyzed, and its frequency or probability?

713. What do you know?

714. What were the Causes that contributed?

715. What can happen?

2.36 Procurement Management Plan: Organizational Infrastructure

716. Are Organizational Infrastructure project contact logs kept up to date?

717. Are any non-compliance issues that exist communicated to your organization?

718. Have external dependencies been captured in the schedule?

719. Have stakeholder accountabilities & responsibilities been clearly defined?

720. Is there a set of procedures defining the scope, procedures, and deliverables defining quality control?

721. Is the current scope of the Organizational Infrastructure project substantially different than that originally defined?

722. Has the Organizational Infrastructure project scope been baselined?

723. Does all Organizational Infrastructure project documentation reside in a common repository for easy access?

724. What areas does the group agree are the biggest success on the Organizational Infrastructure project?

725. Have the procedures for identifying budget

variances been followed?

726. Is there a procurement management plan in place?

727. Does the business case include how the Organizational Infrastructure project aligns with your organizations strategic goals & objectives?

728. Are cause and effect determined for risks when others occur?

729. Does the Organizational Infrastructure project have a formal Organizational Infrastructure project Charter?

730. Is the structure for tracking the Organizational Infrastructure project schedule well defined and assigned to a specific individual?

731. Have all team members been part of identifying risks?

732. If standardized procurement documents are needed, where can others be found?

733. Are target dates established for each milestone deliverable?

734. How long will it take for the purchase cost to be the same as the lease cost?

735. Is the Organizational Infrastructure project schedule available for all Organizational Infrastructure project team members to review?

2.37 Source Selection Criteria: Organizational Infrastructure

736. What should be considered when developing evaluation standards?

737. How should the oral presentations be handled?

738. What are the most critical evaluation criteria that prove to be tiebreakers in the evaluation of proposals?

739. Is experience evaluated?

740. How can the methods of publicizing the buy be tailored to yield more effective price competition?

741. Are considerations anticipated?

742. If the costs are normalized, please account for how the normalization is conducted. Is a cost realism analysis used?

743. What should be the contracting officers strategy?

744. Is a letter of commitment from each proposed team member and key subcontractor included?

745. How much past performance information should be requested?

746. How will you decide an evaluators write up is sufficient?

747. What should clarifications include?

748. In which phase of the acquisition process cycle does source qualifications reside?

749. How do you ensure an integrated assessment of proposals?

750. What should be considered?

751. Does your documentation identify why the team concurs or differs with reported performance from past performance report (CPARs, questionnaire responses, etc.)?

752. When is it appropriate to conduct a preproposal conference?

753. What documentation is necessary regarding electronic communications?

754. When must you conduct a debriefing?

2.38 Stakeholder Management Plan: Organizational Infrastructure

755. Are schedule deliverables actually delivered?

756. Who is accountable for the achievement of the targeted outcome(s) and reports on the progress towards the target?

757. How accurate and complete is the information?

758. What potential impact does the Organizational Infrastructure project have on the stakeholder?

759. Has a capability assessment been conducted?

760. Are staff skills known and available for each task?

761. Is there any form of automated support for Issues Management?

762. What action will be taken once reports have been received?

763. Have Organizational Infrastructure project team accountabilities & responsibilities been clearly defined?

764. Has a Organizational Infrastructure project Communications Plan been developed?

765. Are the results of quality assurance reviews provided to affected groups & individuals?

766. Will all outputs delivered by the Organizational Infrastructure project follow the same process?

767. Do you use diagrams and tables to account for complex concepts and increase overall readability?

768. What specific resources will be required for implementation activities?

769. How will the equipment be verified?

770. Are meeting minutes captured and sent out after the meeting?

771. Is stakeholder involvement adequate?

2.39 Change Management Plan: Organizational Infrastructure

772. Have the approved procedures and policies been published?

773. Who is the audience for change management activities?

774. Is a training information sheet available?

775. Does this change represent a completely new process for your organization, or a different application of an existing process?

776. Readiness -what is a successful end state?

777. What prerequisite knowledge or training is required?

778. How frequently should you repeat the message?

779. What roles within your organization are affected, and how?

780. What risks may occur upfront, during implementation and after implementation?

781. What can you do to minimise misinterpretation and negative perceptions?

782. What tasks are needed?

783. Has this been negotiated with the customer and sponsor?

784. Has the relevant business unit been notified of installation and support requirements?

785. Why would a Organizational Infrastructure project run more smoothly when change management is emphasized from the beginning?

786. What do you expect the target audience to do, say, think or feel as a result of this communication?

787. Change invariability confront many relationships especially the already stated that require a set of behaviours What roles with in your organization are affected and how?

788. Who will be the change levers?

789. What method and medium would you use to announce a message?

790. Clearly articulate the overall business benefits of the Organizational Infrastructure project -why are you doing this now?

3.0 Executing Process Group: Organizational Infrastructure

791. How do you measure difficulty?

792. Mitigate. what will you do to minimize the impact should a risk event occur?

793. Based on your Organizational Infrastructure project communication management plan, what worked well?

794. Have operating capacities been created and/or reinforced in partners?

795. Does the case present a realistic scenario?

796. Will a new application be developed using existing hardware, software, and networks?

797. How will professionals learn what is expected from them what the deliverables are?

798. Is the Organizational Infrastructure project making progress in helping to achieve the set results?

799. What are the critical steps involved with strategy mapping?

800. What are the challenges Organizational Infrastructure project teams face?

801. How do you control progress of your

Organizational Infrastructure project?

802. Do schedule issues conflicts?

803. What are the main parts of the scope statement?

804. Will new hardware or software be required for servers or client machines?

805. What are deliverables of your Organizational Infrastructure project?

806. What business situation is being addressed?

807. What are crucial elements of successful Organizational Infrastructure project plan execution?

3.1 Team Member Status Report: Organizational Infrastructure

808. How does this product, good, or service meet the needs of the Organizational Infrastructure project and your organization as a whole?

809. The problem with Reward & Recognition Programs is that the truly deserving people all too often get left out. How can you make it practical?

810. Does every department have to have a Organizational Infrastructure project Manager on staff?

811. Are your organizations Organizational Infrastructure projects more successful over time?

812. Will the staff do training or is that done by a third party?

813. Are the products of your organizations Organizational Infrastructure projects meeting customers objectives?

814. How it is to be done?

815. How much risk is involved?

816. What specific interest groups do you have in place?

817. Is there evidence that staff is taking a more

professional approach toward management of your organizations Organizational Infrastructure projects?

818. How will resource planning be done?

819. When a teams productivity and success depend on collaboration and the efficient flow of information, what generally fails them?

820. What is to be done?

821. Why is it to be done?

822. Does your organization have the means (staff, money, contract, etc.) to produce or to acquire the product, good, or service?

823. Are the attitudes of staff regarding Organizational Infrastructure project work improving?

824. How can you make it practical?

825. Do you have an Enterprise Organizational Infrastructure project Management Office (EPMO)?

826. Does the product, good, or service already exist within your organization?

3.2 Change Request: Organizational Infrastructure

827. Who is included in the change control team?

828. Can static requirements change attributes like the size of the change be used to predict reliability in execution?

829. Screen shots or attachments included in a Change Request?

830. What has an inspector to inspect and to check?

831. How can changes be graded?

832. Has the change been highlighted and documented in the CSCI?

833. Should a more thorough impact analysis be conducted?

834. What kind of information about the change request needs to be captured?

835. Why were your requested changes rejected or not made?

836. How is quality being addressed on the Organizational Infrastructure project?

837. What is the change request log?

838. How do you get changes (code) out in a timely manner?

839. How does your organization control changes before and after software is released to a customer?

840. What is a Change Request Form?

841. Has a formal technical review been conducted to assess technical correctness?

842. What should be regulated in a change control operating instruction?

843. How fast will change requests be approved?

844. Why do you want to have a change control system?

845. What is the relationship between requirements attributes and reliability?

3.3 Change Log: Organizational Infrastructure

846. Does the suggested change request seem to represent a necessary enhancement to the product?

847. Is the requested change request a result of changes in other Organizational Infrastructure project(s)?

848. Will the Organizational Infrastructure project fail if the change request is not executed?

849. How does this change affect the timeline of the schedule?

850. Is the change request within Organizational Infrastructure project scope?

851. Is this a mandatory replacement?

852. Do the described changes impact on the integrity or security of the system?

853. Where do changes come from?

854. Is the submitted change a new change or a modification of a previously approved change?

855. How does this change affect scope?

856. When was the request approved?

857. Is the change backward compatible without limitations?

858. When was the request submitted?

859. Who initiated the change request?

860. Is the change request open, closed or pending?

861. How does this relate to the standards developed for specific business processes?

3.4 Decision Log: Organizational Infrastructure

862. Do strategies and tactics aimed at less than full control reduce the costs of management or simply shift the cost burden?

863. What are the cost implications?

864. What is the average size of your matters in an applicable measurement?

865. What was the rationale for the decision?

866. It becomes critical to track and periodically revisit both operational effectiveness; Are you noticing all that you need to, and are you interpreting what you see effectively?

867. How does the use a Decision Support System influence the strategies/tactics or costs?

868. At what point in time does loss become unacceptable?

869. Behaviors; what are guidelines that the team has identified that will assist them with getting the most out of team meetings?

870. Is everything working as expected?

871. How consolidated and comprehensive a story can you tell by capturing currently available incident

data in a central location and through a log of key decisions during an incident?

872. How does an increasing emphasis on cost containment influence the strategies and tactics used?

873. How do you know when you are achieving it?

874. How effective is maintaining the log at facilitating organizational learning?

875. Meeting purpose; why does this team meet?

876. Which variables make a critical difference?

877. How do you define success?

878. Is your opponent open to a non-traditional workflow, or will it likely challenge anything you do?

879. What is the line where eDiscovery ends and document review begins?

880. Who is the decisionmaker?

881. How does provision of information, both in terms of content and presentation, influence acceptance of alternative strategies?

3.5 Quality Audit: Organizational Infrastructure

882. How does your organization know that its systems for assisting staff with career planning and employment placements are appropriately effective and constructive?

883. Statements of intent remain exactly that until they are put into effect. The next step is to deploy the already stated intentions. In other words, do the plans happen in reality?

884. Is your organizational structure established and each positions responsibility defined?

885. How does your organization know that its system for examining work done is appropriately effective and constructive?

886. What experience do staff have in the type of work that the audit entails?

887. What mechanisms exist for identification of staff development needs?

888. Are all employees including salespersons made aware that they must report all complaints received from any source for inclusion in the complaint handling system?

889. Does the audit organization have experience in performing the required work for entities of your type

and size?

890. How does your organization know that its relationships with industry and employers are appropriately effective and constructive?

891. Are people allowed to contribute ideas?

892. How does your organization know that its information technology system is serving its needs as effectively and constructively as is appropriate?

893. How does your organization know that its relationships with relevant professional bodies are appropriately effective and constructive?

894. What are you trying to accomplish with this audit?

895. How does your organization know that its Strategic Plan is providing the best guidance for the future of your organization?

896. How does your organization know that its staff entrance standards are appropriately effective and constructive and being implemented consistently?

897. How does your organization know that its advisory services are appropriately effective and constructive?

898. How does your organization know that its planning processes are appropriately effective and constructive?

899. How does your organization know that the

system for managing its facilities is appropriately effective and constructive?

900. What does the organizarion look for in a Quality audit?

901. How does your organization know that its systems for meeting staff extracurricular learning support requirements are appropriately effective and constructive?

3.6 Team Directory: Organizational Infrastructure

902. How will you accomplish and manage the objectives?

903. Have you decided when to celebrate the Organizational Infrastructure projects completion date?

904. Who are your stakeholders (customers, sponsors, end users, team members)?

905. Process decisions: how well was task order work performed?

906. How do unidentified risks impact the outcome of the Organizational Infrastructure project?

907. Where will the product be used and/or delivered or built when appropriate?

908. Process decisions: are there any statutory or regulatory issues relevant to the timely execution of work?

909. How and in what format should information be presented?

910. Where should the information be distributed?

911. Process decisions: is work progressing on schedule and per contract requirements?

912. Is construction on schedule?

913. Does a Organizational Infrastructure project team directory list all resources assigned to the Organizational Infrastructure project?

914. Timing: when do the effects of communication take place?

915. Who will be the stakeholders on your next Organizational Infrastructure project?

916. Who should receive information (all stakeholders)?

917. How will the team handle changes?

918. Process decisions: do invoice amounts match accepted work in place?

919. When will you produce deliverables?

3.7 Team Operating Agreement: Organizational Infrastructure

920. What administrative supports will be put in place to support the team and the teams supervisor?

921. Methodologies: how will key team processes be implemented, such as training, research, work deliverable production, review and approval processes, knowledge management, and meeting procedures?

922. Do you prevent individuals from dominating the meeting?

923. Are there more than two national cultures represented by your team?

924. Are leadership responsibilities shared among team members (versus a single leader)?

925. Do you ask participants to close laptops and place mobile devices on silent on the table while the meeting is in progress?

926. Seconds for members to respond?

927. What types of accommodations will be formulated and put in place for sustaining the team?

928. What is your unique contribution to your organization?

929. Why does your organization want to participate in teaming?

930. Do you post any action items, due dates, and responsibilities on the team website?

931. How do you want to be thought of and known within your organization?

932. Do you vary your voice pace, tone and pitch to engage participants and gain involvement?

933. How does teaming fit in with overall organizational goals and meet organizational needs?

934. Is compensation based on team and individual performance?

935. Are there more than two functional areas represented by your team?

936. Do you use a parking lot for any items that are important and outside of the agenda?

937. What is teaming?

938. Communication protocols: how will the team communicate?

939. Does your team need access to all documents and information at all times?

3.8 Team Performance Assessment: Organizational Infrastructure

940. If you are worried about method variance before you collect data, what sort of design elements might you include to reduce or eliminate the threat of method variance?

941. To what degree are the goals ambitious?

942. To what degree are fresh input and perspectives systematically caught and added (for example, through information and analysis, new members, and senior sponsors)?

943. If you have received criticism from reviewers that your work suffered from method variance, what was the circumstance?

944. To what degree do members understand and articulate the same purpose without relying on ambiguous abstractions?

945. Delaying market entry: how long is too long?

946. When does the medium matter?

947. To what degree can the team measure progress against specific goals?

948. To what degree are the relative importance and priority of the goals clear to all team members?

949. To what degree can team members meet frequently enough to accomplish the teams ends?

950. How do you encourage members to learn from each other?

951. How do you recognize and praise members for contributions?

952. To what degree does the teams work approach provide opportunity for members to engage in open interaction?

953. When a reviewer complains about method variance, what is the essence of the complaint?

954. To what degree do team members articulate the teams work approach?

955. Can team performance be reliably measured in simulator and live exercises using the same assessment tool?

956. What makes opportunities more or less obvious?

957. To what degree do team members understand one anothers roles and skills?

958. If you have criticized someones work for method variance in your role as reviewer, what was the circumstance?

959. To what degree does the teams work approach provide opportunity for members to engage in fact-based problem solving?

3.9 Team Member Performance Assessment: Organizational Infrastructure

960. What variables that affect team members achievement are within your control?

961. Does the rater (supervisor) have to wait for the interim or final performance assessment review to tell an employee that the employees performance is unsatisfactory?

962. In what areas would you like to concentrate your knowledge and resources?

963. What tools are available to determine whether all contract functional and compliance areas of performance objectives, measures, and incentives have been met?

964. What, if any, steps are available for employees who feel they have been unfairly or inaccurately rated?

965. To what extent did the evaluation influence the instructional path, such as with adaptive testing?

966. How are performance measures and associated incentives developed?

967. To what degree does the team possess adequate membership to achieve its ends?

968. How should adaptive assessments be implemented?

969. To what degree can all members engage in open and interactive considerations?

970. How will you identify your Team Leaders?

971. To what degree will new and supplemental skills be introduced as the need is recognized?

972. Who receives a benchmark visit?

973. Do the goals support your organizations goals?

974. How do you determine which data are the most important to use, analyze, or review?

975. What are the standards or expectations for success?

976. What happens if a team member receives a Rating of Unsatisfactory?

977. To what degree are sub-teams possible or necessary?

978. What stakeholders must be involved in the development and oversight of the performance plan?

3.10 Issue Log: Organizational Infrastructure

979. Is the issue log kept in a safe place?

980. Do you have members of your team responsible for certain stakeholders?

981. How do you reply to this question; you am new here and managing this major program. How do you suggest you build your network?

982. What is the impact on the Business Case?

983. Why do you manage human resources?

984. Are stakeholder roles recognized by your organization?

985. Why multiple evaluators?

986. What would have to change?

987. What date was the issue resolved?

988. What effort will a change need?

989. What is a Stakeholder?

990. What is the impact on the risks?

991. What approaches do you use?

992. Do you feel a register helps?

993. Persistence; will users learn a work around or will they be bothered every time?

4.0 Monitoring and Controlling Process Group: Organizational Infrastructure

994. Is the program in place as intended?

995. Does the solution fit in with organizations technical architectural requirements?

996. Is the program making progress in helping to achieve the set results?

997. How to ensure validity, quality and consistency?

998. What is the expected monetary value of the Organizational Infrastructure project?

999. Are the necessary foundations in place to ensure the sustainability of the results of the programme?

1000. How well defined and documented were the Organizational Infrastructure project management processes you chose to use?

1001. What is the timeline?

1002. How can you make your needs known?

1003. How was the program set-up initiated?

1004. Where is the Risk in the Organizational Infrastructure project?

1005. What areas were overlooked on this Organizational Infrastructure project?

1006. Do clients benefit (change) from the services?

1007. Is the schedule for the set products being met?

1008. How is Agile Organizational Infrastructure project Management done?

1009. How do you monitor progress?

4.1 Project Performance Report: Organizational Infrastructure

1010. To what degree will the team ensure that all members equitably share the work essential to the success of the team?

1011. How is the data used?

1012. To what degree are the demands of the task compatible with and converge with the mission and functions of the formal organization?

1013. What is the degree to which rules govern information exchange between groups?

1014. To what degree does the task meet individual needs?

1015. How will procurement be coordinated with other Organizational Infrastructure project aspects, such as scheduling and performance reporting?

1016. To what degree does the information network communicate information relevant to the task?

1017. To what degree can team members vigorously define the teams purpose in considerations with others who are not part of the functioning team?

1018. To what degree can the cognitive capacity of individuals accommodate the flow of information?

1019. To what degree are the teams goals and objectives clear, simple, and measurable?

1020. To what degree will team members, individually and collectively, commit time to help themselves and others learn and develop skills?

1021. To what degree will the approach capitalize on and enhance the skills of all team members in a manner that takes into consideration other demands on members of the team?

1022. To what degree does the funding match the requirement?

1023. To what degree are the demands of the task compatible with and converge with the relationships of the informal organization?

4.2 Variance Analysis: Organizational Infrastructure

1024. Budgeted cost for work performed?

1025. Favorable or unfavorable variance?

1026. Is data disseminated to the contractors management timely, accurate, and usable?

1027. How do you verify authorization to proceed with all authorized work?

1028. How does the use of a single conversion element (rather than the traditional labor and overhead elements) affect standard costing?

1029. Are the bases and rates for allocating costs from each indirect pool consistently applied?

1030. Does the contractor use objective results, design reviews and tests to trace schedule performance?

1031. Budget versus actual. how does the monthly budget compare to actual experience?

1032. How does your organization measure performance?

1033. Does the contractors system provide unit or lot costs when applicable?

1034. Did an existing competitor change strategy?

1035. Contemplated overhead expenditure for each period based on the best information currently is available?

1036. At what point should variances be isolated and brought to the attention of the management?

1037. Is there a logical explanation for any variance?

1038. Are significant decision points, constraints, and interfaces identified as key milestones?

1039. Does the contractors system identify work accomplishment against the schedule plan?

1040. Is the market likely to continue to grow at this rate next year?

4.3 Earned Value Status: Organizational Infrastructure

1041. Where are your problem areas?

1042. How does this compare with other Organizational Infrastructure projects?

1043. Where is evidence-based earned value in your organization reported?

1044. If earned value management (EVM) is so good in determining the true status of a Organizational Infrastructure project and Organizational Infrastructure project its completion, why is it that hardly any one uses it in information systems related Organizational Infrastructure projects?

1045. How much is it going to cost by the finish?

1046. Are you hitting your Organizational Infrastructure projects targets?

1047. When is it going to finish?

1048. What is the unit of forecast value?

1049. Validation is a process of ensuring that the developed system will actually achieve the stakeholders desired outcomes; Are you building the right product? What do you validate?

1050. Verification is a process of ensuring that

the developed system satisfies the stakeholders agreements and specifications; Are you building the product right? What do you verify?

1051. Earned value can be used in almost any Organizational Infrastructure project situation and in almost any Organizational Infrastructure project environment. it may be used on large Organizational Infrastructure projects, medium sized Organizational Infrastructure projects, tiny Organizational Infrastructure projects (in cut-down form), complex and simple Organizational Infrastructure projects and in any market sector. some people, of course, know all about earned value, they have used it for years - but perhaps not as effectively as they could have?

4.4 Risk Audit: Organizational Infrastructure

1052. Are testing tools available and suitable?

1053. For this risk .. what do you need to stop doing, start doing and keep doing?

1054. Mitigation -how can you avoid the risk?

1055. Tradeoff: how much risk can be tolerated and still deliver the products where they need to be?

1056. Do you have an understanding of insurance claims processes?

1057. What are the boundaries of the auditors responsibility for policing management fidelity?

1058. What does your data tell you about your risks?

1059. Does your organization have or has considered the need for insurance covers: public liability, professional indemnity and directors and officers liability?

1060. Does the customer have a solid idea of what is required?

1061. What are the Internal Controls ?

1062. Is your organization an exempt employer for payroll tax purposes?

1063. What resources are needed to achieve program results?

1064. What are the risks that could stop you from achieving your objectives?

1065. What are the costs associated with late delivery or a defective product?

1066. Do requirements demand the use of new analysis, design, or testing methods?

1067. What are the benefits of a Enterprise wide approach to Risk Management?

1068. Do staff understand the extent of duty of care?

1069. Do you promote education and training opportunities?

4.5 Contractor Status Report: Organizational Infrastructure

1070. What are the minimum and optimal bandwidth requirements for the proposed solution?

1071. If applicable; describe your standard schedule for new software version releases. Are new software version releases included in the standard maintenance plan?

1072. What process manages the contracts?

1073. What is the average response time for answering a support call?

1074. How long have you been using the services?

1075. How is risk transferred?

1076. What was the final actual cost?

1077. What was the budget or estimated cost for your organizations services?

1078. Describe how often regular updates are made to the proposed solution. Are corresponding regular updates included in the standard maintenance plan?

1079. What was the overall budget or estimated cost?

1080. Are there contractual transfer concerns?

1081. Who can list a Organizational Infrastructure project as organization experience, your organization or a previous employee of your organization?

1082. What was the actual budget or estimated cost for your organizations services?

4.6 Formal Acceptance: Organizational Infrastructure

1083. Who would use it?

1084. Do you buy pre-configured systems or build your own configuration?

1085. Was the Organizational Infrastructure project goal achieved?

1086. What was done right?

1087. Was the Organizational Infrastructure project managed well?

1088. Does it do what Organizational Infrastructure project team said it would?

1089. Did the Organizational Infrastructure project achieve its MOV?

1090. What function(s) does it fill or meet?

1091. What lessons were learned about your Organizational Infrastructure project management methodology?

1092. Was the Organizational Infrastructure project work done on time, within budget, and according to specification?

1093. Who supplies data?

1094. Have all comments been addressed?

1095. Is formal acceptance of the Organizational Infrastructure project product documented and distributed?

1096. How well did the team follow the methodology?

1097. What features, practices, and processes proved to be strengths or weaknesses?

1098. Does it do what client said it would?

1099. Did the Organizational Infrastructure project manager and team act in a professional and ethical manner?

1100. Do you buy-in installation services?

1101. How does your team plan to obtain formal acceptance on your Organizational Infrastructure project?

1102. Was the client satisfied with the Organizational Infrastructure project results?

5.0 Closing Process Group: Organizational Infrastructure

1103. Specific - is the objective clear in terms of what, how, when, and where the situation will be changed?

1104. Does the close educate others to improve performance?

1105. Can the lesson learned be replicated?

1106. What is the risk of failure to your organization?

1107. Was the user/client satisfied with the end product?

1108. Did you do things well?

1109. Did the Organizational Infrastructure project management methodology work?

1110. What were the actual outcomes?

1111. What level of risk does the proposed budget represent to the Organizational Infrastructure project?

1112. What could have been improved?

1113. What were things that you need to improve?

1114. Is this a follow-on to a previous Organizational Infrastructure project?

1115. How well did you do?

1116. Were the outcomes different from the already stated planned?

1117. Did the delivered product meet the specified requirements and goals of the Organizational Infrastructure project?

5.1 Procurement Audit: Organizational Infrastructure

1118. Are vendor price lists regularly updated?

1119. Does the manual contain policies relating to all business management functions?

1120. Was the estimated contract value in line with the final cost of the contract awarded?

1121. Does the approval include approval of prices?

1122. Were the documents received scrutinised for completion and adherence to stated conditions before the tenders were evaluated?

1123. Was the performance description adequate to needs and legal requirements?

1124. Could the bidders assess the economic risks the successful bidder would be responsible for, thus limiting the inclusion of extra charges for risk?

1125. Are there established procedures for dealing with and documenting non-performance and return of goods?

1126. Are all claims certified by the officer giving rise to the claim (usually the purchasing agent)?

1127. How do you assess whether the technical and financial evaluation was done properly and in fair manner?

1128. In case of time and material and labour hour contracts, does surveillance give an adequate and reasonable assurance that the contractor is using efficient methods and effective cost controls?

1129. Are cases of double payment duly prevented and corrected?

1130. Is the routing of copies of purchase order forms defined?

1131. Is your organization aware and informed about international procurement standards and good practice?

1132. Are buyers prohibited from accepting gifts from vendors?

1133. Does the procurement unit have sound commercial awareness and knowledge of suppliers and the market?

1134. Are required quality and service standards set?

1135. Were all interested operators allowed the opportunity to participate?

1136. Is the approval graduated according to the amount disbursed?

1137. Has your organization procedures in place to monitor the input of experts employed to assist the procurement function?

5.2 Contract Close-Out: Organizational Infrastructure

1138. Parties: Authorized?

1139. How is the contracting office notified of the automatic contract close-out?

1140. Change in knowledge?

1141. Has each contract been audited to verify acceptance and delivery?

1142. Was the contract complete without requiring numerous changes and revisions?

1143. Are the signers the authorized officials?

1144. How/when used ?

1145. Parties: who is involved?

1146. What happens to the recipient of services?

1147. Change in attitude or behavior?

1148. How does it work?

1149. Was the contract sufficiently clear so as not to result in numerous disputes and misunderstandings?

1150. Have all acceptance criteria been met prior to final payment to contractors?

1151. Have all contracts been completed?

1152. Change in circumstances?

1153. Was the contract type appropriate?

1154. What is capture management?

1155. Have all contracts been closed?

1156. Have all contract records been included in the Organizational Infrastructure project archives?

5.3 Project or Phase Close-Out: Organizational Infrastructure

1157. Who controlled the resources for the Organizational Infrastructure project?

1158. What information did each stakeholder need to contribute to the Organizational Infrastructure projects success?

1159. What were the desired outcomes?

1160. Is the lesson based on actual Organizational Infrastructure project experience rather than on independent research?

1161. What was expected from each stakeholder?

1162. What are the informational communication needs for each stakeholder?

1163. What process was planned for managing issues/ risks?

1164. Is there a clear cause and effect between the activity and the lesson learned?

1165. If you were the Organizational Infrastructure project sponsor, how would you determine which Organizational Infrastructure project team(s) and/or individuals deserve recognition?

1166. What is a Risk Management Process?

1167. How much influence did the stakeholder have over others?

1168. Were messages directly related to the release strategy or phases of the Organizational Infrastructure project?

1169. What are they?

1170. Were cost budgets met?

1171. Who exerted influence that has positively affected or negatively impacted the Organizational Infrastructure project?

1172. Have business partners been involved extensively, and what data was required for them?

1173. Who controlled key decisions that were made?

1174. What can you do better next time, and what specific actions can you take to improve?

1175. Does the lesson educate others to improve performance?

5.4 Lessons Learned: Organizational Infrastructure

1176. How well is the build process working?

1177. What were the lessons learned on this Organizational Infrastructure project?

1178. Who is responsible for each action?

1179. How well did the Organizational Infrastructure project Manager respond to questions or comments related to the Organizational Infrastructure project?

1180. How will you allocate your funding resources?

1181. What data are likely to be missing?

1182. How do individuals resolve conflict?

1183. Was the change control process properly implemented to manage changes to cost, scope, schedule, or quality?

1184. How timely was the training you received in preparation for the use of the product/service?

1185. What mistakes did you successfully avoid making?

1186. How well does the product or service the Organizational Infrastructure project produced meet the defined Organizational Infrastructure project requirements?

1187. Was sufficient time allocated to review Organizational Infrastructure project deliverables?

1188. How much communication is task-related?

1189. Are there any hidden conflicts of interest?

1190. What are the Benefits of Measurements?

1191. What is the growth stage of your organization?

1192. What is the fiscal dependency?

1193. Are corrective actions needed?

Index

excellence   8, 41
excellent   59
except 158
excess 157
excessive   204
exchange   246
exclude   91
executed   227
Executing   6, 153, 209, 221
execution   105, 153, 190, 222, 225, 234
executive   8, 117
exempt   252
exercise   26
exercises   239
exerted   265
existence   211
existing 12-13, 99, 120, 135, 151, 219, 221, 249
expect 119, 146, 177, 182, 220
expected   27, 35, 89, 110-111, 132, 141, 175, 189, 221, 229, 244, 264
expense   157
experience   126-127, 177, 198, 203, 215, 231, 248, 255, 264
experiment   121
expertise   141, 181
experts 41, 195, 261
explained   12
explicitly   118
explore   67
exposure   205
exposures   86
expressed   142
extent 13, 18, 22, 25, 39, 85, 139-140, 240, 253
external   31, 58, 128, 213
facilitate   13, 23, 71, 96
facilities   233
facing 19, 123
fact-based   239
factor 146
factors 92, 117, 139, 186, 207
failed 54
failing 205
failure 55, 115, 137, 212, 258
fairly   40

provide   21, 65, 118, 121, 126, 136, 175, 179, 185, 192, 239, 248
provided   9, 14, 105, 137, 144, 199, 217
providers   86
provides   147
providing   98, 136, 151, 166, 187, 232
provision   143, 230
public 140, 252
published   219
publisher   1
pulled 118
purchase   10, 12, 214, 261
purchased   12
purchasing   260
purpose   2, 12, 129, 135, 151, 172, 185, 230, 238, 246
purposes   141, 252
pushing   112
qualified   40, 61, 66, 73, 76, 144, 160, 175
qualifies   69
qualify 47, 66
qualities   21
quality 1, 4, 6, 12, 27, 54, 59, 65-67, 69, 86, 95, 104, 111, 179, 182, 187, 189-191, 193-194, 197-199, 213, 217, 225, 231, 233, 244, 261, 266
quantified   101
quantify   47
question   13-14, 18, 30, 46, 61, 78, 94, 107, 128, 242
questions   8, 10, 13, 76, 201, 266
quickly 13, 62, 64, 73
radically   69
rapidly 175
rather 51, 125, 248, 264
Rating 241
rational   157-158
rationale   229
reached   23
reaching   129
reactivate   111
readiness   36, 200, 219
readings   98
realism 215
realistic   23, 70, 161, 207, 221
reality 231

relate 71, 174, 228
related 25, 68, 102, 202, 250, 265-266
relating   188, 260
relation   21, 23, 81, 129
relations   128, 205, 210
relative 101, 190, 238
relatively   113
release 146, 154, 181, 265
released   226
releases   254
relevant   12, 32, 46, 65, 99, 125, 153, 190, 200, 208, 220,
232, 234, 246
reliably 239
relying 238
remain 45, 231
remaining   186
remember   178
remunerate   84
repeat 219
rephrased   12
replace   52
replanning   159
replicated   258
Report 6-7, 80, 89, 98, 206, 216, 223, 231, 246, 254
reported   145, 152, 158, 216, 250
reporting   66, 99, 123, 158-159, 246
reports 46, 103, 136, 144, 161, 175, 183, 196, 203, 217
repository   213
represent   81, 187, 219, 227, 258
reproduced   1
reputation   110
request   6, 76, 187, 200, 225-228
requested   1, 91, 215, 225, 227
requests   200, 226
require 33, 56, 65, 72, 99, 105, 157, 170, 205, 220
required   20, 23, 31, 36-37, 39, 43, 56, 58, 67, 74, 85, 89-90,
104, 132, 145, 158, 162, 178, 180, 198-199, 201, 218-219, 222, 231,
252, 261, 265
requiring   136, 262
research   25, 114, 117, 138, 151, 236, 264
reserved   1
reside 92, 213, 216
resolution   65, 90

resolve 20, 24, 266
resolved   132, 191, 242
resource   4-5, 111, 139, 153, 160, 170, 172-175, 199, 224
resources   2, 10, 22-23, 26, 28, 40, 51, 89, 98, 104, 109, 111,
118, 126, 132, 135, 137, 158, 162, 164-165, 172, 175, 177, 181,
186, 195, 199, 218, 235, 240, 242, 253, 264, 266
respect   1
respond   140, 195, 236, 266
responded   14
response   21, 25, 97, 99, 101-103, 254
responses   127, 206, 216
responsive   178, 185
result   72, 81, 87, 151, 185, 220, 227, 262
resulted   97
resulting   71, 141, 159
results   10, 33, 35, 48, 63, 78, 80-82, 84, 86, 89-90, 92, 101, 105,
132, 139-140, 142, 186, 189, 191, 217, 221, 244, 248, 253, 257
Retain 107
retained   74
retention   47
retrospect   118
return 87, 122, 194, 260
returns 191
revenue   27, 56
revenues   60
review 12-13, 36, 58, 71, 141, 168, 180, 189, 191, 206, 214, 226,
230, 236, 240-241, 267
reviewed   45, 152, 154, 191, 205
reviewer   239
reviewers   238
reviews 12, 161, 174, 182, 189, 217, 248
revised 74, 97, 158
revisions   262
revisit 229
reward 52, 59, 76, 223
rewarded   27
rewards   96
rework 49
rights   1
robustness   166
routine 104
routing 261
rushing 201

stretch 116
strict 70
strive 116, 176
striving 134
strong 175
Strongly   13, 18, 30, 46, 61, 78, 94, 107
structure   3-4, 56, 80, 113, 120, 152, 155-156, 172, 179, 214,
231
Structured   109
stubborn   112
stupid 113
subdivided   195
subject 10-11, 41
subjects   76
submit 12
submitted   12, 227-228
subset 18
sub-teams   241
subtotals   183
succeed   55, 121
success   21, 31, 37, 39, 43, 55-57, 82, 85, 89, 98, 107-108,
114-115, 117, 122-123, 125, 132, 137, 160, 184, 203, 207-208, 213,
224, 230, 241, 246, 264
successes   114
successful   65, 87, 95, 115, 119-120, 132, 139, 187, 219, 222-
223, 260
succession   104
suffered   238
sufficient   139-140, 157, 215, 267
suggest   210, 242
suggested   103, 187, 227
suitable   252
summarize   174
summary   175, 196
supervisor   236, 240
supplier   87, 117
suppliers   41, 70-71, 124, 261
supplies   161, 256
supply 55, 166
support   8, 26, 73, 95, 97, 101, 108, 126, 132, 137, 160, 170,
197, 209, 217, 220, 229, 233, 236, 241, 254
supported   69
supporting   85, 98, 161, 190

CPSIA information can be obtained
at www.ICGtesting.com
Printed in the USA
BVHW081416250719
554363BV00016B/1524/P